INSIDE
BROADMOOR

I0795329

Jonathan Levi is a successful television executive and BAFTA-nominated documentary film maker. Attracted to the extremes in society, he was the first person to ever gain full access to the patients and staff at Broadmoor for a highly-acclaimed primetime ITV series offering startling insights into the minds of some of Britain's most notorious psychiatric patients.

When TV star and recording artist Tulisa was entrapped by the *Sun on Sunday* she turned to Jonathan to author and tell her story for BBC1 in the ratings hit *Tulisa: The Price of Fame*. Jonathan has made programmes with Andrew Lloyd Webber about his art collection and his musicals, and has hosted fundraisers with The Old Vic.

He was Factual Producer on ITV four-part drama, *Hatton Garden*, and co-authored a book on the same subject, *Hatton Garden: The Inside Story*.

Dr Emma French writes about how particular people, places and stories hit the headlines and capture the public imagination. Her books include *Selling Shakespeare to Hollywood*, and, as Co-Author with Jonathan Levi, *Hatton Garden: The Inside Story*. She lives in London with Jonathan and their three children.

INSIDE BROADMOOR

Up close and personal
with Britain's most
dangerous criminals

JONATHAN LEVI

& EMMA FRENCH

BLINK
bringing you closer

First published in the UK by Blink Publishing
An imprint of Bonnier Books UK
80–81 Wimpole Street, London, W1G 9RE
Owned by Bonnier Books
Sveavägen 56, Stockholm, Sweden

facebook.com/bonnierbooksuk/
twitter.com/bonnierbooks_uk

Paperback – 978-1-788700-94-8
Ebook – 978-1-788700-95-5

British Library Cataloguing-in-Publication Data:

A CIP catalogue of this book is available from the British Library.

Typset by seagulls.net

Printed and bound in Great Britain by Clays Ltd, Elcograf S.p.A.

9 10 8

John Blake Publishing is an imprint of Bonnier Books UK
www.bonnierbooks.co.uk

This book is dedicated to all victims and to their families. Writing this book has taught us the difficult truth that it is possible to be both a victim and a perpetrator.

Contents

All names of any current living patients have been changed for their privacy and protection and to safeguard victims' families.

This book is entirely the views of the authors, based upon extensive research and not the official view or opinion of Broadmoor Hospital or its governing body West London NHS Trust.

Prologue

There would be plenty of time for questions later.

For now, the nurses and security were intent upon breaking the lethal nine-hour barricade inside the little corner of hell that resident murderer Robert 'Bob' Maudsley had created. Bob and his companion, David Cheeseman, had sealed themselves inside with a third patient, David Francis, a known paedophile. He had apparently riled Bob and David Cheeseman by conducting a homosexual attack on one of their friends. Inside sources had reason to believe, though, that their preference if opportunity had presented was to 'go for a member of staff'.

David Francis had been hog-tied with a record player flex and tortured throughout the interminable deadlock in the claustrophobic, airless unit. Burly and grizzled as the Broadmoor male nurses tended to be back then, they could not break inside Bob Maudsley's room. Eventually, put out of his agony with a makeshift garroting, he was then paraded in front of the cell's spy hatch for the helpless Broadmoor staff to see.

When they finally gained access, the victim was partially skinned. This flaying had likely taken place while he was still alive, as his screams echoing through Broadmoor during his ordeal had testified. One of the first nurses on the scene described to us 'sperm coming out of every orifice' of the victim; the nurse is still traumatised by the experience, decades later. According to another staff source quoted in the press, David Francis was discovered with his head 'cracked open like a boiled egg', a spoon hanging out of it and his brain partially absent.

More than 40 years on, this 1977 incident remains perhaps the most notorious crime to take place within Broadmoor's walls – and there is certainly plenty of competition for that dubious honour. As one staff member put it, 'they moved intensive care from Monmouth to Norfolk [wards]. Both patients are still alive, but not at Broadmoor. They went to court and got prison terms. They should have been returned to Broadmoor. But the incident changed practice.' Understandably, staff past and present still pore over every detail.

How it happened. Why it happened. Whether it could ever happen again.

Introduction

'The public perceive this place as just being
rapists, murderers and paedophiles. But some
of us are in for self-harm, burglary and then
we got ill in prison. We get tarred with the
same brush, and the public think we are all
monsters. And it's not fair.'

– Broadmoor patient

Broadmoor. Few place names in the world have such profound and chilling resonance. For over 150 years, it has contained the UK's most violent, dangerous and criminally insane mental patients, including paedophiles, killers and cannibals. In 2019, it is also where just under 200 highly vulnerable men call home.

Perched on a hill above the picturesque village of Crowthorne, Broadmoor looms large, both in its Victorian Gothic architecture and in the public's imagination. When most people think of Broadmoor, they think of its more infamous inmates: Ronnie Kray, Charles Bronson, Peter Sutcliffe, Kenneth Erskine. Legends for all the wrong reasons. Many of these patients were inmates during the 1980s, Thatcher's Britain, when Broadmoor was at its most notorious, and the hospital was always in the tabloid press.

But Broadmoor is changing, evolving, as it has always done over the years. Soon, the hospital will move to a new set of buildings. Whether or not it retains its reputation as the most dangerous secure facility remains to be seen, but during our time spent interviewing inmates and staff, we soon came to see that the patients aren't two-dimensional villains, or legends crying out to be emulated. No, the truth about Broadmoor is far more complex and interesting than that.

Broadmoor is a sprawling campus, with numerous buildings spread over a large area and surprisingly beautiful gardens with a stunning view of the surrounding countryside – not that you'd choose to stay there. As one patient we met said, 'It's a great view, but it never changes.'

The main car park to Broadmoor is always full, so we tend to park in the overflow car park, near the site where the new hospital is going to be. An A4 sheet of paper needs to be filled out with NHS VISITOR and the registration plate clearly written down and displayed on the dashboard. We have never seen a parking attendant in all of our many visits, but each time we have conscientiously filled out this form. Huge construction machines squat stolidly nearby and site tarpaulins flap in the wind. It very often rains in this exposed part of Berkshire. There are many trees, mainly miserable, spindly specimens.

The walk from the visitors' overflow car park flows through a path and into some woods. It feels like a walk into an activity centre but there are no bike riders, no children in pushchairs or on scooters. Once you've heard the escape stories, it is hard not to shiver with fear here.

At the summit of the steep hill comes the first close-up of the red-brick wall. Beside it is an empty building, with cramped, freezing toilets. From there it's a one-minute walk to the main entrance of the hospital. Once there was a grand entrance with a clock tower and a Victorian archway. It's still there, but now is on the back of the building, out of service and disused, and in its place is a bland, municipal-style front entrance.

Electric glass doors slide open at your approach and to the right are some small, transparent Perspex lockers. Rather like a doctor's surgery, the reception in the centre is clinical, with posters on the walls and paperwork to fill out. Unlike a doctor's surgery, a glass screen separates visitors from the reception staff, the posters are of prohibited items, and to the left is an airport-style X-ray machine for bags and an X-ray archway to walk through. The reception is often unattended and when someone from security comes back to their desk they at times seem baffled that there is a visitor.

The security guards may look casual but watch your every move. Photos are taken, fingerprints cross-checked on high-tech scanners and keys are passed through so that all your possessions can be placed in one of the lockers. They are mostly always full and iPhones, car keys and handbags line up, displayed but locked away in these odd little see-through cupboards.

There is a long list of restricted items. You pat yourself down, questioning yourself: do I have a CD case in my pocket I forgot about? A pad of paper with a metal wire binding? Do I have sharp keys or a penknife? It is the same flash of fear as approaching 'nothing to declare' at an airport on the way home. An unfounded but insistent sense of guilt.

Coats come off and are placed in the tray provided. You are patted down by a security guard holding an electronic paddle that glides up and down near your body, scanning for hidden weapons or anything else potentially hazardous in such a high-risk environment.

Once we had become known as regulars to the security staff, this part of the process involved a bit of banter, but they never stopped taking their job deadly seriously. The smallest error at this point is, after all, a matter of life and death in Broadmoor.

Once in, there are some hints as to why Broadmoor intends to move house very soon. On a December visit, sleet dripped through a huge hole in the ceiling, where two tiles had completely disintegrated. It plopped insistently into a blue plastic bucket, a makeshift solution that contrasted oddly with the incredibly high-tech security.

When you have retrieved your coat and put it on, you can walk, phone-less, key-less, and weapon-less through, another set of doors into a dank and depressing waiting room. There, you await the key-jangling staff member whose job it is to collect you that day.

The waiting room has a bolted-down sofa, red with black circles. On the wall is an embroidery, made by a patient who spent time in Broadmoor between 1939 and 1963: *Showing the Panorama from Seven, Broadmoor*. It had been presented sometime around the year 1960 to Dr W.S. Maclay, a psychiatrist and medical member of the Board of Control. Many years after Dr Maclay's death, it was rediscovered by his son, rolled up in a cardboard tube in the attic of his family house in Kensington.

Dr Maclay's son returned it to Broadmoor, where he felt it belonged. It shows the view from Cornwall House, which was demolished in the 1980s. On a table, wildlife magazines lie alongside a copy of the Gideon's New Testament and Psalms. Many have found God here.

Finally, an escort arrives to take you through a series of airlocks and vast metal internal gates, a CCTV camera trained on you all the while, before you come to the final gate, which will let you into Broadmoor Hospital. The security is, of necessity, extremely tight, designed to be virtually impossible to break into the hospital, as well as breaking out of it. We've often mused on how we might get into Broadmoor by nefarious means – fake fingerprints, hypnotising staff, all very unlikely *Mission: Impossible* stuff – but the fact is that any attempt to break in would be thwarted at the final door, which is operated via the security cameras. All of this has the result of making you feel as if you're in a different world, which, to all intents and purposes, you are. Broadmoor is not your typical high security institution, and the patients and the staff are not typical people.

It can feel like a ghost town inside the wall. It's sometimes hard to believe that 200 of Britain's most dangerous men live here, with many hundreds more of staff and security. Quite often it feels empty. This is because of the strict rules around patient movement. Cameras record where each patient is at any given moment. Patients who are well enough and are living on assertive rehab wards leave their bedrooms to work, go to therapy and even go shopping.

Broadmoor's wards are broken down into different, rather quaint British place names as well as, of course, into differing levels of patient illness and violence levels. They are Ascot Ward, Cranfield Ward, Harrogate Ward, Newmarket Ward, Sandown Ward, Woburn Ward, Canterbury Ward, Dover Ward, Folkestone Ward, Kempton Ward, Chepstow Ward and Epsom Ward. It all sounds frightfully genteel, like a day at the races rather than a maximum security hospital.

There are the red-brick Victorian buildings. It is hard to see where one starts and one finishes. They appear to be attached to one another and you walk in what feels like circles to come to small locked doors in the corners of these buildings. There are low-rise, unattractive modern buildings too. The wards are homes to the patients and the workplaces of the staff. It is hard, however, to process this fact as you approach and enter one of them. That some of the men in this poky claustrophobic place have lived here day in, day out, with no break or trip outside for decades.

The big clock that sits above the original entrance to the old hospital is stuck at just after six, and it will never tick again in this place. Inside Broadmoor, you have the feeling that time has slowed right down; the clock may have slowed to a complete halt, but the lives and aspirations of the patients have slowed down too. Perhaps this is appropriate. Many of these men have taken lives. Almost all off them are here because of extreme violence, sex offending or fire setting.

Every time you forget for a moment where you are, something reminds you what a bizarre and peculiar environment you are in. Watching men get searched and patted down every time they go from A to B, walking into the woodwork and craft areas and seeing each pair of scissors, each stapler, each sharp object with its own holster and home, each one counted in and out each time they are used and moved around the workshop.

Some of the men amble and mumble; some of them are manic. Dr Gwen Adshead, one of the most experienced psychiatrists on staff, memorably told us that the patients' lives shrink when they get to the hospital. Whatever they were before, a husband, a worker, a member of a golf club or a political party, it has gone. The old them is dead; the new them is a patient. And not just any patient, but a Broadmoor patient. Even if they are eventually released, that will always stay with them. As a result, they simultaneously seem to grow and also to shrivel. They grow simply because of their terrible diet and lack of exercise; they shrivel as their world becomes very small.

Broadmoor's 200 patients are all men considered to be suffering from mental disorders. They are all classified as vulnerable adults. 'I have done everything from taking hostages, stabbings, fire settings, I set fire to the first psychiatric hospital I was sent to,' one patient called Alan told us when we asked what he was like when he was not on medication. 'I am very violent and paranoid, I come close to attacking people as I think people are going to attack me and I don't want to get attacked first. I spent 11 months in segregation without my medication because I was too dangerous to come out.'

Each one of these men costs the taxpayer upwards of £300,000 a year to live in this place. Each one has their own daily schedule, therapy regime and complex medication requirements. Each one has their own terrible history. Seventy per cent come from prisons and the court system, 25 per cent from medium secure psychiatric units and the remaining 5 per cent includes transfers from other high secure UK hospitals, such as Rampton and Ashworth. Broadmoor's patients are all men suffering from mental disorders who present a grave and immediate risk to the public. Many have committed violent crimes, from arson to torture, rape and murder.

That these men are classed as vulnerable may come as a surprise to many people. Of course, while the hospital would prefer people to come in with an open mind, whether they choose to admit it to themselves or not, anyone on their first visit to Broadmoor will have certain preconceptions, which come mainly from the media. Many think that Broadmoor is simply the dumping ground for society's most notorious criminals. A final destination with no hope of return. They are wrong.

Former clinical director, Dr Amlan Basu said, 'The easiest reaction in the world is to see someone who has committed something atrocious, label them as evil and want to lock them up and throw away the key.' Staff working at Broadmoor, however, have to believe in redemption, or at least rehabilitation.

Throughout this book, we explore the complex relationship between the patients and those dedicated staff who are tasked with stepping into the dark waters of their minds. The patients' stories, while sickening and frightening, are ultimately, we hope, about trying to bring both patient and clinician to a point of understanding of the crime that's been committed. What did they do, why did they do it, and will they do it again? Maybe sooner than we're expecting? As the Robert Maudsley case shows, just being incarcerated, especially at that time, did not guarantee anyone's safety, including the patient's own safety.

Can clinicians and their elite teams unravel the mysteries of their patient's past and their brain chemistry to try and make them 'safe'? Can everyone be rehabilitated or are some conditions simply untreatable? Is there really such a thing as evil? We explore the psychology of both the patients and those tasked with caring for them. What draws people to this work, what keeps them there, how does it change them, and what is the impact on those around them?

How do we treat those we're scared of, those we don't want to become, but are endlessly fascinated by? What can we do with those who are a danger to themselves and others and may never recover? Are we treating these men or just containing them? These are the most dangerous people our society has ever produced. The word 'choice' is deliberate – society has produced these people, and the vast majority of them came from homes where they were treated appallingly. If being incarcerated means that they are paying a debt to society, does society owe them anything in turn? There are no easy answers to these questions, and perhaps there shouldn't be, perhaps raising the questions and exploring what the answers might be is enough.

As you go back through the security gates and collect your possessions from the Perspex containers, as you walk towards the car park and towards your car, as you leave Broadmoor behind, it is almost impossible to resist the temptation not to google the men you met that day on your smartphone as soon as you leave – it's human nature. That guy you met in the kitchen on an assertive rehab ward whose younger face then looks out at you in newspaper articles and court reports? 'Cannibal', the headlines scream. That guy who stopped you in the corridor and said something weird and creepy turns out to be a paedophile and a murderer.

The truth is that Broadmoor is made up of many different stories, from troubled young men to staff members whose family has worked in the hospital for generations. It is the story of people who have harmed others, and the people who want to help them. It is the story of the truth behind the legends, the facts behind the media frenzy, and the reality behind the myth.

Chapter 1

History

Until Jonathan had been allowed in to make a TV series in 2014, Broadmoor had been closed to the scrutiny of cameras and its 800 staff members were warned not to discuss patients outside the hospital walls. Partly because of this – and partly due to the many high-profile cases brought to the public's attention by the media – Broadmoor, out of all the high security hospitals in Britain, has always had a hold on the public's imagination.

Most people we spoke to about the book think of Broadmoor as a prison, isolated on a windswept heath somewhere miles from any human habitation. Far from it. Broadmoor is a hospital on the eastern edge of a bustling and populous village just 40 miles from central London. In keeping with the oddly rural and idyllic connotations of the name Broadmoor, there are several local nature reserves. South of the village on the way to Sandhurst, which shares its name with one of the Broadmoor wards, is pretty Edgbarrow Woods. On the northern edge of Crowthorne is a site of Special Scientific Interest,

Heath Lake, and a second such site, Sandhurst to Owlsmoor Bogs and Heaths, including Wildmoor Heath, can be found in the south-east. These quaint fairy tale places belie the fact that they've acted as a haven for many of Broadmoor's escaped killers over the decades.

Crowthorne is pleasant enough, slightly old-fashioned and down-at-heel. A packed Lidl car park lies at its centre, often the scene of minor road rage incidents as locals slip into disputed spaces, jumping the queue and provoking stand-up rows outside the budget supermarket. The village has precisely all the stuff you would expect. Fish and chip shop, betting shop, butcher's, Chinese takeaway. Completely unexceptional and ordinary in every way except one.

Crowthorne is a civil parish in the south-eastern Berkshire district of Bracknell Forest, forming part of the Reading/Wokingham Urban Area. Today, it has a population of about 7,000 people, but in the mid-19th century, it was a tiny hamlet until a couple of momentous arrivals put it on the map.

The renowned public school, Wellington College, opened in 1859. Wellington eventually gave rise to one of Crowthorne's few local celebrities outside Broadmoor's walls, Sir Anthony Seldon, political biographer and Headmaster of Wellington College. A year later, the opening of Crowthorne railway station marked the landmark of public mass transport coming to Crowthorne for the very first time. Then, of course, Broadmoor opened its gate in 1863. This activity prompted a period of rapid growth for the village.

The first inmates of Broadmoor were 95 women who arrived in 1863, most of whom had killed their children while suffering post-natal depression. It was first built as a Victorian lunatic asylum for the criminally insane.

Broadmoor was founded on idealistic and often forward-thinking principles. These early patients all went through some standard experiences upon admission: a medical examination, an interview with a doctor and then off to the admissions ward. Treatment involved fresh air, labour, exercise and regular meals. For many, having experienced the horror of life as the Victorian poor, the asylum was exactly that – a genuine and therapeutic refuge from the hardships of the world outside. Hardships which in many cases might have fuelled their mental illness or criminal acts. One innovative treatment was the 'rhubarb treatment', in which patients were fed an average of 50 pounds of rhubarb annually. Although the programme of drug therapy was virtually non-existent compared to modern Broadmoor's use of pharmaceuticals as part of the therapy process, sedatives were used.

There was just one female block, which had taken less time to build than the five male blocks. Those were completed and opened in February 1864, bringing some notorious inmates, including the celebrated artist Richard Dadd, who had killed his father, and Edward Oxford, the failed assassin of Queen Victoria.

Writing in 1903, George Griffith described the place: 'The only likeness that Broadmoor bears to a prison consists in the fact that you can go nowhere without the unlocking and relocking of solid doors and iron gates; but within these there is no evidence of restraint. In the male wing you see men lounging about the long, airy corridors, or sitting in the big, well-furnished, common rooms, reading, smoking, looking out of the windows, or sitting motionless, thinking the thoughts and dreaming the dreams of a world that is not ours.

'So, too, in the female wing there are women sitting about the corridors, knitting and doing lacework or embroidery, or, like the men, sitting in their common rooms, reading or talking, or also thinking those strange thoughts. In another room you will find one at a grand piano, playing, it may be, some standard piece of music, or it may be some weird creation of her own, and others sitting about on the chairs and lounges listening to her.'*

Then, as now, Broadmoor had a very lively cultural and spiritual life. Victorian Broadmoor hosted regular dramatic productions and concerts. Male and female patients were carefully segregated, but the women were allowed to hold a female-only dance once a fortnight. The amount of thought that the new Broadmoor Hospital has put into its new visitor centre harks back to the hospital's very earliest days, when the families and friends of patients were welcomed.

The Mental Deficiency Act was introduced in 1913 to replace The Idiot's Act of 1886. The Act, now a tasteless relic of pre-war Britain, distinguished between four categories of people who should no longer be in the mainstream prison system. These were 'Idiots – People so "deeply defective in mind

---

* George Griffith, *Sidelights on Convict Life*, London: John Long (1903)

as to be unable to guard against common physical dangers"', 'Imbeciles – Able to protect themselves from common dangers, but not capable of caring for themselves. Imbeciles were thought of as more intelligent than idiots, but still incapable of managing themselves of their affairs' and 'Feeble-Minded Persons – More intelligent than an imbecile, and therefore able to support themselves to some extent, but with "defectiveness" still "so pronounced that they require care, supervision, and control for their own protection or the protection of others"'. There was another vague category just called 'Moral Defects', who displayed some form of 'mental defect' alongside 'strong vicious of criminal propensities on which punishment had little or no effect'.

The fundamental aim of the Mental Deficiency Act was to remove the mentally ill from prisons and poor houses and place them in specialist 'mental deficiency colonies'.

The idea of colonies was based on Winston Churchill's now breathtaking proposal to the House of Commons in February 1911 that those who were thought to be 'mentally defective', according to a report he had read nearly 150,000 people, should work in forced labour camps.

In addition to being guilty of a crime, anyone deemed to fall into any of the four categories above could also be placed in one of the colonies if they were thought to be homeless, abandoned, neglected, unschoolable, or habitually drunk. At one point, these criteria led to almost 65,000 people being placed in colonies or other institutions. Many of these people were simply convicts, who were free to leave when their prison sentence expired, and not considered to pose a lasting danger to the general public.

For the first 50 years of its existence, Broadmoor was the sole facility of its kind serving England and Wales, until Rampton opened its doors in 1912 to service the North of England.

In 1959, the Mental Deficiency Act, and the Lunacy and Mental Treatment Acts, were replaced by the Mental Health Act. The biggest achievement of the Act was removing the legal distinction between mental deficiency and mental illness. The main direct implication for Broadmoor was that it became possible to admit non-offenders for the first time, acknowledging a proactive approach to those with 'dangerous, violent or criminal propensities'.

From 1863 to 1949, Broadmoor was a criminal lunatic asylum under the Home Office. During that time, a medical superintendent was in charge of the daily administration of the hospital. When Broadmoor Criminal Lunatic Asylum became Broadmoor Institution in 1949, it was vested in the Minister of Health and placed under the management of the board of control, but also still administered by a medical superintendent. Then, in 1960, it came directly under Ministry of Health management as a 'special hospital for mentally disordered persons who in the opinion of the Minister require treatment under conditions of special security on account of their dangerous, violent or criminal propensities'.

Of course, as with any institution, the culture was driven by those in charge even more so than by these changing government acts. The 1895 appointment of a prison medical governor, Dr Richard Brown, drove patient numbers up and saw a much stricter regime. His two successors, however, Dr Baker and Dr Sullivan, had a more humane approach, taking the feel back towards more of an asylum than a prison by offering greater chance of work, play and for patients to engage in their own treatment.

Many staff and patients speak of not just Crowthorne but of Broadmoor itself as a village. This quaint and startlingly odd terminology might at first be taken as ironic. In actuality, it seems intended to tame the notion of Broadmoor as a volatile and violent environment, alienating and atomised. There is a saying, 'There is time and then there is Broadmoor time'. For the less unwell, who are acutely aware of their surroundings, it is often agonisingly slow.

Patrick McGrath is a writer, whose father Pat McGrath became Broadmoor's last superintendent in 1957. McGrath and his family lived in an expansive Victorian villa near the Main Gate, which his parents named Kentigern after the patron saint of Glasgow where they'd grown up. Kentigern came complete with a pond, grounds, servants' quarters and so on. Patrick McGrath had friendships with parole patients, and he also described patients being employed in a series of artisan workshops, and staff versus patients sports days.

As a child growing up on the Broadmoor campus, he had a level of interactions with patients that is jaw-dropping now. McGrath visited Broadmoor again, many years later, and was struck, as many others have been, by the taming and corporate blandness creeping into the place, with lawns and offices replacing wild spaces and his childhood home.

He was disturbed by the walls, fences, floodlights and control room. The cash shelled out on the high-tech set of barriers would have been better spent on patient care, he felt. Maybe McGrath's childhood Broadmoor was brilliant at the gentler bits of therapy and care, but its security levels to modern eyes look woefully dodgy.

Gwen Adshead is a psychiatrist and a doctor who has lived and breathed Broadmoor for 30 years. Gwen is a Christian, and someone who believes that evil acts exist. Her memories of Broadmoor stretch back to the eighties.

'I remember visiting when I was still a very junior doctor, having only just completed basic training in psychiatry. I remember that I visited Broadmoor on what was a regular open day during the week when members of the public and professionals could visit for an afternoon. The afternoon began with a talk and then an escorted trip around the hospital, looking at various wards and workshops. I remember the feeling of anticipation as I had the same fantasies as everyone else and found the idea of Broadmoor to have a Gothic quality, with its dark brick walls and its forbidding nature.

'I remember the first time feeling incredibly naive and being patronised by the nurses who worked there, who were in fact all members of the Prison Officers' Association; and acted very much as prison officers wearing uniform that had epaulettes and badges. They very much took the approach that the visitors knew nothing and had to be protected from their own naivete.

'Like the patients, we were corralled and had to walk around in a crocodile, like school, with restrictions on what to do and what not to do. I remember that we were taken to see one of the men's workshops, where the men were making bricks and we saw the women's workshops, where the women were sewing. I remember that my friend and I both found visiting the hospital oppressive and found the sexism of the workshops very dispiriting. We went to the pub afterwards and felt very gloomy about Broadmoor as a place and I remember feeling glad to get away and having a strong sense that it would be professionally unethical to work in such a repressive and authoritarian kind of place.'

In those days, in the early to late eighties and early nineties, Broadmoor was not a popular place for consultants to work. As a result, all the colleagues there had massive workloads; one colleague of Gwen's notoriously had 70 patients. To put that in perspective, the number now is more like 20.

Gwen recalls 'the nursing staff wore long white coats and wore peaked hats as well; they expected the patients to address them as Mr so-and-so whereas they would address the patients by their Christian names. It was not unusual for patients only to see the consultant once or twice a year, although there were other non-consultant doctors (often from India) who saw patients more frequently and who attended to their physical health. I remember the ancient paper files which went back ages; and were very thick; the average length of stay in the hospital was about 10 to 13 years because there was less expectation that people would leave the hospital.' Those were the days before the expansion of secure psychiatric services so there was nowhere for them to go.

'I remember the very busy workshops: the carpenter's, the picture framer's, the bricklayer's and the electrical shop. I remember the Central Hall with its stage where the Broadmoor Players used to put on the annual panto with amusing jokes about the staff and doctors. I remember that there were 500 men and 100 women, who would occasionally meet at discos which were closely supervised like a school dance. I remember hearing the screams and yells on the female side and how silent the male side was in contrast.

'I remember walking up and down the terrace, which gave the most beautiful view of three counties. I remember thinking that it was sad that people who came to the hospital and saw this view would never go out and how generous it was of the architects to give them a view to look at. Later, I realised that people would leave the hospital and seeing the view gave them inspiration and hope. I remember the education centre and how busy it was, with men doing a variety of exams and lessons, and the kindness of the staff there. I also remember the wonderful kitchen gardens where the hospital once used to grow all the fruit and vegetables that the inmates would need (including an astounding amount of rhubarb in the early years). However, when I went to the hospital first the kitchen garden still provided work for patients, raising fruit and plants for sale. It was a lovely place to be; there were also animals: goats, rabbits, birds.

'I remember the language of the hospital and how the nurses used to refer to themselves as staff or staff men. I remember that I was firmly told that I was "not staff" and how I was told that I could not work or walk around the hospital without someone knowing where I was at all times. I remember receiving the message that the nursing staff really owned the hospital and every ward was a kind of individual fiefdom.'

As the 1980s myth goes, admission to Broadmoor was granted only to members of an exclusive club of the criminally insane. When Gwen Adshead arrived, Yorkshire Ripper Peter Sutcliffe was there, convicted in 1981 of murdering 13 prostitutes; Kenneth Erskine, the Stockwell strangler who murdered seven elderly people in 1986, is still there; and London nail bomber David Copeland, who targeted blacks, Bangladeshis and gays, killing three people and injuring 129, of whom four lost limbs, has also spent time in Broadmoor.

In the 1970s and 80s, Gwen explained, people were given mental health disposals who wouldn't do now. 'I am thinking of a man who, aged 18, broke into an elderly lady's home and raped and murdered her. A nasty offence. And he went straight to Broadmoor. If you did something that was nasty and weird back then, you would go straight to Broadmoor. The thinking was not terribly sophisticated back then: if

you had done something weird, you must be mad.'
Now, however, there are far fewer people being
diagnosed as criminally insane, and those who once
would have been admitted to Broadmoor, are now
incarcerated within the general prison population.

The world is changing, and Broadmoor is changing too. For example, the number of beds has
dramatically reduced. At one point Broadmoor had
over 1,000 beds, now it has just 200. We spoke to
former clinical director Dr Amlan Basu, who is very
concerned that this particular myth, about Broadmoor functioning as a long-term dumping ground
for incurable psychopaths, is busted: 'There is still a
public perception that when you go to Broadmoor,
you are there for life, but the high-profile individuals
that are there for decades are outliers.'

Broadmoor is certainly a place with a great deal
of myth and misunderstanding surrounding it. Its
genesis as a criminal lunatic asylum that offered
precious little hope of any return to normal life
lingers to this day. But, as we will see, Broadmoor
offers hope to its patients, the hope of rehabilitation
and the hope of one day returning to the outside
world a changed person.

Chapter 2

Staff

The staff of Broadmoor are hugely talented individuals. They compete for roles at this most prestigious and fascinating of hospitals for the criminally insane. For individuals working in the field of personality disorder and paranoid schizophrenia, a job at Broadmoor can be a major aspiration.

The history of nursing at Broadmoor is a chequered and fascinating one. There can be few aspects of the hospital which have changed so radically over time.

Clive Bonnet is now retired, but he used to run the Prevention and Management of Violence and Aggression department. A nurse by background, he has gained an extraordinary amount of clinical experience over more than 30 years' service. He is third-generation Broadmoor. He grew up on the neighbouring Broadmoor estate, which still houses many of the staff today. Clive has lived on the estate all his life and he knew a lot of the nurses from his earliest childhood.

His grandad started at Broadmoor in 1918 and worked there for 32 years. Clive's dad had his first day back in 1946 – and lasted for an impressive 46 years. Clive's brother worked there. Clive himself started in 1974, so he had spent 37 years at Broadmoor when we first spoke to him in 2011. There's no doubt that he offers a unique historical angle. In person, he looks really tough: jeans, shaved head, goatee, tattoos, Chelsea boots, functional glasses.

When Clive was growing up, the estate 'was like a mining village. Your domestic and career relationship was based around Broadmoor. It was almost where you were destined to be.' Though it could have the feel of a charming, sleepy English village, external security was extremely important. He recalls the familiar refrain, 'Get away from the wall, young Bonnet!'

Clive's dad was the senior nursing officer and a well-known figure. 'You're Tony Bonnet's son,' people would say, and you had to put on a front. Clive only ever took one half-day sick at Broadmoor and that was when he dislocated his finger in an 'incident'. He is deeply loyal to both his father's memory and to the institution itself: 'I am most proud of making Dad pleased. He shed a tear when he retired. Nobody in my presence would knock Broadmoor.'

Clive's first day on the ward was as an 18-year-old, when he was put onto the Adolescent unit. As he recalls it, he felt no anxiety, just a lot of interest. No nerves, but lots of questions. There was an undeniable mystique – 'I wonder what's behind the wall' – and suddenly, the mystique lifted. He felt comfortable, safe, in competent hands. After all, they were all members of a truly unique team.

Clive's second day, on the middle ward of Norfolk House, saw him asked to sit down, and he was given the patients' case notes. Back then, they all did that on a regular basis. They were taught from day one to study the patients. Why were they there? What was the diagnosis? In those days they had crime-scene photos in the case notes on admissions, which they don't have access to now. They were encouraged to find a way of understanding who the patients were, but they were also constantly reminded to be mindful of how very dangerous their charges could be. 'They're not here for stealing Smarties!' was the stock phrase.

While the era of Clive's early days at Broadmoor sometimes sounds shockingly fast and loose compared to now, he was very keen to emphasise that there have always been stopgaps. As he said, 'When I started, you couldn't do intensive care for six months minimum, because it was disturbing and you had to prove yourself first.' Although 'the first day was in civvies', he believes in staff wearing a uniform. He recalls and admires what was once a staff mantra: 'Always look after the blue shirt' – the uniform. Nowadays, however, staff do not wear a uniform, and he feels the loss of it now.

Clive spent most of his time on the intensive care unit. Hostage situations were quite common; they had formal training on riots. The intensive care unit at the time had major structural downfalls, namely very long corridors, and iron gates added because of a hostage scenario.

Clive worked in other environments too. He was on Gloucester House for some time, a semi-paroled, institutionalised block. Patients were even given little allotment gardens there.

Over the years, Clive has seen so many staff come and go: 'Some people are straightforwardly not up to it. One type realises straight away, lasts a week. The person who isn't up to it but *doesn't realise* it hides in the toilet. I've known two people like that. Then there are the people who say it's not affecting them.'

Clive said that this latter category could become extremely anguished, as negative feelings and fears are internalised. In some extreme and tragic cases, it has led to staff suicide.

But, on the other hand, the staff at Broadmoor share a strong bond. As Clive fondly put it, 'You can never forget the camaraderie. Some staff are your friends but *all* are your comrades! The gallows humour is a coping mechanism.'

Decades of care have granted him deep psychological insights, but the eternal truth appears to be that the only thing you can predict is the unpredictable.

'You don't know what's coming out. When you lock up and when you open up are the most dangerous times. Locking the door at the end of the night breaks the rapport that you have established with the patients.' That can be dangerous.

'After a massive incident you need a sugary cup of tea, you are shaking with adrenalin.' Following the very worst incidents Clive witnessed, in place of the sugary tea they would go to the pub. As he put it, even after witnessing the most extreme scenes, 'You worried about your own credibility in terms of admitting weakness.' It was all very stiff upper lip.

Clive never went to staff support once. He received no counselling or support after major incidents: 'That was considered a sign of weakness.

The cup of tea was a post incident debrief.' The change seemed to drift in when it arrived, and better pastoral care came in after some incidents of staff self-harm.

Working in Broadmoor is not just about dealing with the incidents though. There are a number of other skills that you have to marshal too. You can never guarantee that you can control somebody, but you can mitigate risk.

In Clive's view you 'have to break down barriers and establish rapport.' He is proud of his unique job; proud of the historical milestones of the institution, such as the fact that the Prison Officers' Association was established at Broadmoor.

Clive is not in touch with any former patients. That is a big no-no. If an ex-patient came within a ten-mile radius of the hospital that was closely monitored. The patients can be subdivided into different types. Clive described a 'mix': 'Some patients had no insight into their condition. There are some institutionalised patients. And there are some patients who spent years plotting their escape.'

He recalls the good points of more relaxed interactions with patients too. Patients used to be allowed to come out and sweep. They had an attendant with them, but it gave them a sense of freedom and vocation.

In Clive's view, 'human rights' was a major disaster. Previously, the focus had been all about trying to reintegrate a person into the community. Now, patients can have TV whenever they want, but there was a lot to be said for the old system of pay and reward.

Clive revealed that Heathrow used to donate confiscated cigarettes to Broadmoor. In those days, patients could smoke. They would do a chore and get a cigarette: 'Patients cleaned all the wards when I started. There were no domestics. Patients did it! At 9pm, the TV and radio used to go off. As a patient, you could work down in the kitchen gardens. Is it reality to let patients lay in bed all day like they do now? Can you lay in bed until 11am in the real world?'

These days, there has been a definite move towards removing the institutionalised patients. Clive pointed out, though, that it can be cruel to expel them if they don't want to go. If a patient set fire to a hayrick in 1952, and spent decades subsequently in Broadmoor, how do they reintegrate into the real world? When Clive started in 1974, there were patients there from the 1930s.

Another long-term member of staff is Pat McKee, a practice development nurse. A kind, reassuring and compassionate man, his firm handshake told us that he's no pushover. He is strikingly self-effacing and diffident, and rather shy: 'I've got the most boring career of anyone you will speak to.' But Broadmoor nursing is a career that takes place 'behind a 30-foot wall'.

Pat's very first role on joining Broadmoor at age 21 was as a nursing assistant. Like many other Broadmoor old-timers, he intended to come for a short time but then enjoyed it and ended up staying for decades. 'There won't be any more generations who work their whole lives here,' he pointed out to us. Like Clive, Pat's father worked at Broadmoor. Pat is very highly attuned to change over the generations.

We asked him why some staff have stayed for so long. Historically, Broadmoor was a local employer during a time when many people commuted, so it was accessible and local. Many staff were ex-military, in search of 'something that provided a uniform and a house.'

Pat is as struck by the weird eccentricity of 1980s Broadmoor as everyone else. When he started in 1982, there was 'a very militaristic uniform, it was all very regimented'. As we've said, there are no uniforms now. Even so, there are some constants that he was keen to emphasise: 'There has never been a straitjacket, never been a padded cell.' We were surprised by this information, a key myth in Broadmoor's notorious history, that, in fact, has never been the reality.

In Pat's view the core of nursing is all about reading a situation correctly, and he has a great phrase to describe it: 'Gastrointestinal psychiatry – just a gut feeling!'

These days, he is so attuned to patient care that he notices the smallest change in behaviour immediately. It wasn't always that way, though. In the early days he would panic and run to the staff nurse, 'and they would almost always be smoking a roll-up'. Times certainly sound more relaxed then!

Pat was keen to note that 'putting someone behind a 30-foot wall changes their behaviour. Patients are not dissimilar to us'. Patients become unsettled, disorientated, unpredictable. For this amongst other good reasons, each of the shift handovers has *a lot* of detail.

Pat has disseminated some of his key learnings more broadly. He has been involved with a new UK programme for offenders with dangerous and severe personality disorders, who pose a risk of serious harm to others to improve their access to mental health services. Pat has been working closely with the Home Office, Department of Health and the Prison Service, and the patients involved have all perpetrated a violent or sexual crime and have been detained under the criminal justice system or current mental health legislation.

Broadmoor was one of two high secure units to serve as test cases in this rather controversial initiative, which was aimed squarely at protecting the public more effectively and improved patient management and treatment.

Security is obviously a core feature of Broadmoor's day-to-day operations. Pete Turner is a violence reduction specialist and the PMVA Operational Lead High Secure Services at Broadmoor Hospital. Committed, slightly intense, and, very justly, proud of his achievements and where he has got to from being 'the boy behind the wall' to his current broad national role, he's got a brooding, handsome look, and a very direct gaze. He was a training manager then he had a clinical role. Then he took on an overarching role.

Pete is part of an extraordinary five generations of Turners who have worked at Broadmoor. His son works there now, as did three generations before him. Pete has held many significant clinical roles during his impressive career. He started in January 1991, so when we met, he was approaching his thirtieth year at Broadmoor.

Like Pat McKee and Clive Bonnet, Pete was raised on the Broadmoor estate as a child: 'I grew up all my life wondering what was behind the wall.'

His father worked for Broadmoor for 45 years as a charge nurse. As Pete said, 'My dad has a strong value base. Christian. He was badly assaulted, had his teeth knocked out … although that was not on the ward.'

Pete surprised us by using the unexpected word 'oasis' to describe Broadmoor when he first joined. He recalls it being very clean and tidy, with only the long-gone uniform really giving it away as an institution.

In his view, the media plays a big role in developing and driving people's perceptions of Broadmoor, and he swats away the sensationalism, protective of his patients and their extreme vulnerability: 'We are not here to judge. People are here to be cared for.'

That said, Pete acknowledges that the public certainly has a right to know what happens at Broadmoor. He believes they now have a fairly consistent message about rehabilitation, yet even early visitors were surprised and had their expectations reversed.

'We strike a balance between security and clinical. We have always had the balance.'

Pete describes the buildings as 'A mix. Victorian. Eighties. The Paddock. The Victorians had it right – huge windows with lovely views. We've learned from mistakes made with the eighties buildings and paddocks. Big windows. Natural light. Open area. Green space.'

Broadmoor, he recalled, used to be very self-sufficient. When it was male and female they used to have big social functions and discos: 'We still do this stuff but on a smaller scale. No more sports, for instance.

'When I started there was a leather shop, a carpentry shop, pottery shop and print shop.' There was a shop outside the hospital selling what patients made. The philosophy was to provide people with a meaningful day. You would get paid and you could spend it on cigarettes in the canteen. Patients got £90 a week benefits then. Perhaps even more importantly, they could socialise and interact.

'We've lost the full-size snooker tables. Are we too risk-averse now?'

In terms of his field – violence reduction – there used to be what Pete termed 'conveyor-belt trainers'. One-size-fits-all individuals who were not taught to modify their training to fit each patient's needs. He wanted to 'bridge the gap'. Consequently, all his trainers now are attached to the clinical team. Thanks to his good work, he now oversees the standards for the entire NHS trust. Pete also oversees standards for Prevention and Management of Violence and Aggression for the whole of the UK. He presented it to the board, then NHS England and Department of Health.

Pete had some observations on the changing nature of the patient population that he has witnessed in his long service: 'Bad/mad/sad – not that many people are really unwell, or over-medicated.' There are certainly more prison admissions. The stay time has reduced to five years on average: 'People used to be longer-term here. Now there's a high turnover.' The focus of rehabilitation has grown massively, and he is very sensitive to patients' boundaries, saying that, 'I wouldn't go into a patient's room unless absolutely needed or invited. If you go into a patient's room, you need to give treatment.'

Pete has seen a vast improvement in Broadmoor since his arrival in the nineties, from the old-fashioned 'lock 'em up and throw away the key' mentality to rehabilitation. He even has an ex-patient working for him as a trainer!

We were very lucky to be able to discuss the changing nature of therapy in Broadmoor with one of its longest-serving and most thoughtful staff members. We first met Dr Gwen Adshead in 2006 when filming a television documentary about the relationship between madness and creativity. Back then, she showed us some of the artwork created by Broadmoor patients and talked about the links between madness and creativity. In between then and now, Gwen has had her own episode of *Desert Island Discs*, has been writing and teaching but mostly doing what she does best: helping vulnerable patients (at Broadmoor and other institutions) get better.

According to Gwen, what we now see at Broadmoor is almost unrecognisable from the institution that it was at the start of the 1980s. And the move to the new hospital site will create even further distance from the Broadmoor of her early career.

'A lot of the information about the hospital in this eighties era had been transgressively obtained. There is a fascinating parallel between the transgressive nature of the patients, doing something wrong, but the images we have of the hospital from this time are illicitly obtained so we end up having transgressive images of something that doesn't really exist.'

Trangression is a huge theme for Gwen. It is, of course, the reason why the patients are there in the first place, because they have transgressed in some way. But there are other sorts of transgressions too – like how the media obtained information on the patients, and then how that information is written up.

There is almost a comic thread here, she explained. The difference between what is written in the newspaper and what is reality on the ward. Broadmoor is meant to be the mad place but then the newspapers print all of this rubbish so what is madder?

'I have certainly had many men say to me from inside the wall that they read the newspapers and it seems very dangerous out there. That this world inside the hospital is calm and safe and well ordered. And I would rather stay here, it is secure, everyone keeps the rules. Out there, it is lawless with attacks in

the street and I don't know anything about comput-
ers. Why would I want to go out there?'

This period of the hospital – the seventies and
the eighties – also fascinated Gwen as it was a time
where there was still a strong sense of community, at
and around the hospital gates. Something that in her
view is now long gone.

'Very often you still had three generations of families who worked at Broadmoor. People were trained
to work at Broadmoor in Broadmoor by people who
lived on site. It was a local industry.'

One of the fascinating things about Broadmoor,
she explained, is that 'whatever these guys had done
on the outside, they are very rarely interested in
pursuing it on the inside. So the hospital is like a
small town, and like most small communities, the
vast majority of people keep to the rules all the time
and only a very small number are bouncing off the
walls and hitting people, the majority are just getting
on with things, not breaking the rules or even trying
to get around the rules.'

As Gwen said, in patient forums often the topic
of conversation might be 'access to the toast' and
is indicative of people in a long-stay institution and
what becomes important to you. We were all equally

taken by this contrast between the high secure environment and the most banal domestic details.

Gwen emphasised the great vulnerability of very unwell patients too.

'There are quite a few patients who get to Broadmoor because of repeated self-harm as prisons just can't deal with it. The thing that the prisons can't tolerate is people killing themselves. Prisons are running scared of people hurting themselves in prison. So, if I am serving a life sentence for armed robbery in prison and start harming myself, they will want to send me to hospital because of the fear of me killing myself. Because self-harm is both an indicator of suicidal feeling and also a way of releasing distress, you get an awful lot of people self-harming in prison.

'It is hard to understand how peripheral us psychiatrists are to the life of the hospital.' She explained somewhat self-deprecatingly that the real life of the hospital is on the ward. The consultants, the various therapists visit and come in and out but then they leave and the ward goes back to normal. It is, of course, where those people live: 'One of the most important things we managed to establish over the last 20 years is that there are no "private spaces" in the hospital. You don't have privacy between patient and therapist. Therapists supervise each other and it is much better that way.'

Therapy itself has significantly changed since Gwen started at Broadmoor, and this can be seen in the way that immigrants with a surgical background were treated when they came to Britain.

'These were guys who often wanted to come to this country to work as surgeons but couldn't get jobs, mainly for racist reasons, so they found themselves being offered jobs in psychiatry. These doctors were often from India and Uganda and had trained in medicine and often surgery and were really high-quality people who often found themselves pushed into either general practice or psychiatry as these were the only jobs going. So there were often some very interesting characters who were treated in quite a racist and stereotypical way.'

It often used to be, according to Gwen, that the Indian doctors were very keen on medication and the younger female psychiatrists more interested in talking therapy. This was in contrast to more entrenched, traditional views: 'A lot of the white male psychiatrists of this time were quite hang 'em and flog 'em types. If you had right-wing views and were a bit of a control freak you might be drawn to forensic psychiatry. An iron-fisted approach, but seen as a safe pair of hands by the establishment and the Ministry of Justice.'

She explained how involved the civil servants in government were in this phase of the hospital's story.

'If Mr So and So needed to go to the dentist you had to write to the Ministry of Justice and say Mr So and So needs to go to the dentist and wait for their response. And then you had to contact them whenever you wanted to move someone. And the Ministry of Justice very swiftly had a keen sense of the psychiatrists at the hospital as being either "restrainers" or "keeper-inners" and very focused on risk, or whether they were hopelessly liberal "letter-outers".'

Gwen described herself as a 'hopeless letter-outer': 'The patients didn't get reviewed very often. In the bad old days, some of these patients might only be seen twice a year by a psychiatrist. Not like now, where you get a review every three months. The public vision was that people were there for good.'

In her career, she has witnessed the seismic shift from red-brick asylum lock 'em up forever through to the modern 'treatment-focused' approach.

Regarding changing patient numbers, Gwen observed that, 'When I first went there, there were 700, by the time I became a consultant, there were 550 and now it is around 200. The people that come to Broadmoor now are not the high offending psychopaths that you might expect to see in Broadmoor. They are often very disorganised, very damaged men. There is a trickle of the weird and the wonderful but it is much less common than it was.'

She said to us rather memorably, 'I often think that my patients are like survivors of a disaster, where they were the disaster.'

Forensic psychiatrist Dr Amlan Basu is a good-looking, self-effacing and charming individual, and a former clinical director of Broadmoor. Since leaving Broadmoor, he has worked as medical director for the Huntercombe Group, as well as holding a visiting research contract with the Institute of Psychiatry, Psychology and Neuroscience at King's College London. He also serves on the executive committee of the Forensic Faculty at the Royal College of Psychiatrists. His charismatic persona and crisp articulation of his research has led to advisory roles on *Silent Witness* and *Luther*.

Forensic psychiatry deals with mentally disordered people whose actions have led them to be admitted into a high security hospital, such as Broadmoor. It involves a good knowledge of the law in relation to mental health issues.

Amlan had not thought about forensic psychiatry as a career until he practised it as a trainee at the prestigious Maudsley Hospital in South London. There, he became fascinated by the medical and legal aspects of forensic psychiatry, although as he was keen to reassure us, 'I didn't have an odd childhood interest in serial killers!'

At the Maudsley, he spent three years as senior house officer, then three years as a specialist registrar. His particular interest during those years was focused around child/adolescent/forensic psychiatry.

Amlan's first encounter with Broadmoor came when he was a medical student trainee. On that first tour of Broadmoor, he didn't dream that was where he would work eventually. Even so, as he put it, there is 'no getting away from the history of the place, the name resonates with anyone who has grown up in Britain. At the end of your rotation, you have to go where the job is. It was perfect timing because an opportunity at Broadmoor came up.'

Amlan started on a rehabilitation ward in September 2009, where he was a consultant forensic psychiatrist. He then spent six years mainly on high dependency and intensive care wards: 'That is the end of the road as far as security goes – there is nowhere more secure for them to go.' On those wards, he had no choice but to learn very quickly. Then it was back to rehab work because that was less intense and could therefore combine with a management role.

Broadmoor has two different major directorates, split somewhat artificially, into mental illness and personality disorders (see Chapter 3 for more on this split). At the time, he had no ambition to be clinical director. However, he enjoyed the mental illness directorate and running that so much that after a few months the clinical director role came up and he wanted to go for it.

It is clearly a priority for Amlan not only to treat mental disorders, but to challenge misconceptions over how mental illness functions, and how an institution like Broadmoor is able to help patients manage their symptoms. As clinical director of Broadmoor and beyond, he has worked tirelessly to destigmatise and alter the perception of severe mental illness, as well as to enhance the public's understanding of its causes and treatment.

We asked Amlan whether every patient could be cured, or whether there were some who would always reoffend.

In his view, you can only diagnose treatability on a case-by-case basis: 'These are resource-heavy interventions. You need to be judicious about at what point you say, "We have tried everything we can".'

As Broadmoor is a hospital and not a prison, many of its patients can and do move back out into the community. As Amlan described to us, the average stay at the hospital is really down to under six years now.

Amlan explained that Broadmoor patients have shown a notably lower repeat offending rate than the UK prison population overall. This is a far cry from the damaging myth that when you arrive at Broadmoor, they throw away the key and that's your lot for life.

During their time patients are exposed to an intensive programme of drug and psychological therapies. Depending on their response to that treatment a patient might expect to move on to another, medium-secure facility, and ultimately, back out into wider society. In that sense, Broadmoor is of course just one bit of a wider forensic psychiatric care system that seeks to identify and treat people suffering from a mental disorder.

Amlan was proud to be part of a movement that was very keen on radically changing Broadmoor's culture from a prison mentality to recovery and reducing risk. Overall, there is now a hugely over-whelming consensus about the ethos of the hospital being recovery-focused. As we've seen, prison offi-cers now no longer wear uniform, which for Amlan is a huge step forward. There has to be an element of procedural security – there are keys jangling as you walk through the site, but they try to keep it to a minimum. It's part of a broader effort to make the hospital as patient-centred as possible. The patients have to feel it is their home for four to six years.

This level of care and negotiation with patients carries other liabilities though. Amlan put this point very seriously: 'Yes, it's your home but it is a pretty expensive home for the taxpayer – you have certain obligations. Namely, to get the patients to the mind-set that the best route out is the interventions.'

Amlan doesn't skirt away from difficult issues when we press him on them during our book research. On restraint and forced medication – two of the more controversial aspects of mental health

– he is pragmatic. More often than not, talking to patients can encourage them to take their medication. The very difficult decision to use force comes when not only has the patient become a risk to themselves by refusing medication, but a second approved doctor, independent of the hospital, has also signed off on the need for forced medication.

In Amlan's view, the pendulum is certainly swinging towards as little blanket restrictions as you can make. This enhances and improves individual autonomy. That's part of the healing process. 'The ethos, I think, is right where we try not to offer blanket restrictions – there are enough restrictions on people's liberty already in a secure hospital.' It can't be about forcing people to engage in psychological interventions – there's a huge spectrum of differing needs and attitudes.

Amlan misses Broadmoor. 'It's difficult for a place like that to have not infected you in a positive way. My memory of it is very positive. An awful lot of positive teamwork. Some very good clinical leaders at board level. 'You don't miss the security and the processes,' he laughed.

When we talked to Pete Turner, he told us a fascinating story: 'We once had a frightened commissioner who wanted to leave the ward after five minutes. The patients take over the ward sometimes!'

We asked Amlan Basu about this, and he was quick to leap to the Commissioner's defence: 'The environment is so niche. What is the benchmark? If there are only a couple of other high secure hospitals to visit and inspect, what does "good" look like?'

It's an interesting question – what does 'good' look like in an environment such as Broadmoor? Do we have to change our expectations of what good is, when confronted by people who are both criminally insane, yet vulnerable at the same time?

Broadmoor inspires deep loyalty in its staff, many of whom also see the need for constant improvement. It is a place where myth collides with reality, and we constantly had to reassess what we assumed about Broadmoor. It is a place of contradictions, where the most violent are the most vulnerable, and where the horror of the patients' crimes – against themselves and others – is set against the mundane life of the wards. And it is the wards that we will visit next.

Chapter 3

Admissions

There is no doubt that the wards on Broadmoor now are a very different place from the wards of years gone by. In the mid-1960s, for example, it would have been hard for an institution with nearly 1,000 male and female patients, often staying for a decade or even two decades, to imagine an all-male institution with a patient population of less than 200 in 2019.

Massive improvements in psychological treatments, and medication for psychosis and depression have taken place. Throw in game-changing research into neuroimaging and brain chemistry, and a higher recognition of the true therapeutic value of leisure pursuits and manual work, and you have a seismic shift.

One of the most interesting revelations made to us was that your day-to-day behaviour as a patient very much determines where you live in the hospital. So, it truly determines what your life is like.

What never varies is that every new patient spends their first three months on Admissions. This time period involves a really deep look into the patient's history, the nature of their illness and their key treatment requirements. This period of comprehensive assessment does involve treatment, but is also a prelude to when the real treatment begins, typically, but not always, on a high dependency ward. As Dr Amlan Basu explained to us even though every patient is assessed on an individual basis, patients are divided into two broad categories, personality disorders and mental illnesses such as schizophrenia. Some doctors do not even believe that the distinction is a helpful one, but broadly speaking, personality disorders are characterised as an enduring pattern of inner experience that are different from society's expectations of what is normal. For example, anti-social personality disorder, narcissistic personality disorder and borderline personality disorder. Mental illnesses, on the other hand, are things like schizophrenia and depression. To simplify enormously, it is easier to treat mental illnesses with drugs and talking cures than it is to treat personality disorders, which often are life-long, incurable and just have to be managed.

What is and what isn't mental illness isn't so easy to pinpoint as perhaps you'd expect. In fact, it can also be quite fluid – as Dr Amlan Basu said to us, there is a historical perspective to the diagnosis of mental illness. The criteria for mental illness have changed over time. Just a few decades ago, homosexuality was classified as a mental disorder. On the other hand, some things are decidedly constant. By the time we reached the 18th century, most people had adopted a medical perspective on madness and saw it rooted in the same general kinds of pathology as illness. Before then, in medieval times, for instance, there was a belief that Christianity could cure mental torment.

Development of attitudes and research to mental illness is a globalised and ongoing process, so improvements in England affect treatments in other countries and vice versa. Originally known as Pilgrim State Hospital, Pilgrim Psychiatric Center opened in 1931 and was the largest hospital in the world. At its height, it held 13,000 patients, and was renowned for experiments with shock treatments such as insulin shock therapy and electro-convulsive therapy. The asylum became a place of great despair and misery for thousands of patients. It's now far smaller than it once was, predominantly due to the Tarasoff case, which not only revolutionised the face of mental health in the US, but had a corresponding impact on institutions in the UK.

Dr Gwen Adshead told of one such case in the United States – the Tarasoff case – where the ramifications of the events there have had a huge, ongoing impact on the way mental illness is treated today, have changed the law and invigorated mental health research.

Tatiana Tarasoff was a student at Berkeley University, California. In 1968, she met Prosenjit Poddar at folk dancing classes. While the two went out for a bit after this, Tarasoff broke it off after Poddar became too invested in the relationship. Poddar took this badly, falling into a depressive episode, and began to stalk her. In 1969, Poddar told his university counsellor that he was considering murdering Tarasoff.

While the university counsellor tried to get campus police to detain Poddar under the belief that he might be suffering from paranoid schizophrenia, he was immediately released after presenting as sane and denying that he had ever considered killing Miss Tarasoff. Poddar's counsellor was then ordered by his supervisor not to detain Poddar again, as he regarded telling the campus police as a breach of confidentiality. Three weeks later, Tatiana was dead, Poddar having stabbed her with a kitchen knife. While he was initially convicted of second-degree murder and served five years, he was later released on the condition that he return to India.

Tarasoff's mother sued the university. She argued that her daughter should have been protected and that the university counsellors should have been more forthcoming in breaching confidentiality and should have driven for Poddar to be detained, and that Tarasoff should have been warned directly of the threat. In response, it was argued that confidentiality was the bedrock of therapy.

The case was considered so significant it was heard twice by the Supreme Court of California. It was concluded, at last, that confidentiality was not absolute, and that therapists have a duty to protect third parties who are in serious danger of violence from a patient. This led to what has became known as the duty to protect, and the duty to warn. That the need for therapists to protect the public was of greater significance than client-patient confidentiality was a landmark ruling.

The Tarasoff case was instrumental in instigating an outbreak of research into links between mental illness and violence. This research continued into the 1990s, with one of the prime and fairly consistent findings being that the link between mental illness and violence had, in the past, not only been misunderstood, but overexaggerated. Put simply, for a person to commit an act of violence does not mean that they have to be mentally ill. This was an enormous finding that led to a marked shift in how criminals were processed.

Where once the nature of their crime might have automatically initiated a referral to Pilgrim State Hospital, they became more likely to be referred to prison, as mental illness had to be proven, not assumed. Following this drop off in referrals, the Pilgrim Psychiatric Center is only a third of the size of what the Pilgrim State Hospital once was. The significance of this research was also felt in the UK. Many of those who once would have been referred to Broadmoor now go straight to prison.

'The vast majority of people with mental illness don't commit acts of violence,' Dr Gwen Adshead says. 'So to be mentally ill and commit acts of violence is unusual. Another thing that is unusual is that long-stay residential care is going out of fashion all over Europe. The other thing is that the people who are going to Broadmoor now are no longer those people who are doing the really strange things. Of course, there are exceptions.'

She explained that she is working with a man who is serving a whole life tariff and there are lots of concerns about his mental health: 'They ask me what I think. I have no idea. What do you say to someone where the State has decided they will spend their whole life in prison? I don't know what that is like.'

There is a complexity around the differing modes of admission to Broadmoor. Many individuals are joint-managed by Broadmoor and the prison system.

It is not uncommon for an individual transferred to Broadmoor from prison, after becoming unwell there, then to be treated for mental illness for a bit before moving on. If the court decide a hospital order is the most appropriate setting, the patient will go to a hospital that can manage their mental illness. Some serving a prison sentence become profoundly unwell. They are treated at Broadmoor and then returned to prison.

Each patient on arrival is greeted by a staff member, who is able to fill them in on which ward they will be on and more general information about Broadmoor. The patients will be made aware that they might have to share toilets and washrooms, but each of them will have their own room. Once they get to their ward, the patient meets their primary nurse, who will be their key worker while they remain on the ward they've been allocated to.

Patients come in wearing their own clothes, which can necessarily lead to some slightly awkward conversations about whether they're wearing anything unsafe, such as belts, including belt buckles or jewellery. Security is at the forefront from day one. Likewise, most furniture in patients' rooms is secure for their own protection. Really unwell patients aren't allowed many personal possession or keepsakes because of the dangers these can pose to the patient and to others. The timing of the ward tour and a meet and greet with the other patients takes place on a case by case basis, depending on how mentally unwell the patient is when they are first admitted.

Because the services inside Broadmoor are split into two basic pathways, mental illness and personality disorder, all patients are sorted accordingly. The mental illness admission wards are Newmarket ward and Sandown wards, with 12 beds each. Kempton ward, which also has 12 beds, is the admissions ward for personality disorder services. Once they have been admitted to their wards, few of these new arrivals fully realise that they are being watched, judged and monitored 24/7. Depending on how assaultive or self-harming they are, they then get put into one of three sets of wards: intensive care, high dependency or assertive rehab.

Jimmy Noak, deputy director of nursing at the hospital and a warm and charming man, freely acknowledged to us that admissions is often really challenging, because patients can arrive in an extremely paranoid, violent, disorientated or psychotic state. They are likely to be coming from places where the quality of speciality care is inevitably not as high as that at Broadmoor, and even the journey itself may have heightened their mental illness and instability.

Jimmy Noak used to work far more than he does now in admissions. The time was when he would see the full write-up of what people had done to get into Broadmoor every time someone was admitted. Jimmy said that you have to shut yourself off from their crimes or you couldn't treat them. We asked if that compartmentalising was a skill that you learned or if he had it when he started. Jimmy thought about that hard for a minute, turning it over in his mind. Then he shook his head: 'I'm not sure.'

Even in the context of our reading on Broadmoor admissions over the years, a particularly distressing and sickening crime had been committed by a patient who died recently, in 2017. Patrick Reilly committed a horrific crime even by Broadmoor's standards, and his family could not be found after his death.

Reilly was Broadmoor Hospital's longest-serving patient at the time of his death on 6th October 2017. He had lived there for 33 years. In his early twenties he was acquitted of the sexually motivated murder of seven-year-old Leonie Darnley. The jury who declared him innocent did not know of his previous history of rapes and indecent assaults and sobbed when his offences were read out to them at the end of the trial. He did subsequently receive three life sentences for a number of horrific crimes.

Earlier in the year of his death the Crown Prosecution Service appealed at the High Court to quash his acquittal and put him back on trial for the killing of Leonie after the double jeopardy law was dispensed with. At Reading Coroner's Court on 27th November, it was revealed that the 56-year-old had died of oesophagus cancer and had requested not to be resuscitated.

It felt to us that Patrick Reilly would be one of the patients whose crimes you'd have to shut yourself away from in order to treat them. We asked this question of the executive director of the hospital, Leeanne McGee, over a veggie curry in the hospital staff canteen. The staff canteen feels like a total anomaly, a haven of buzzing conversation, plates of chips and banks of soft drinks set within the extraordinary atmosphere of Broadmoor.

Leeanne, a striking, pragmatic, Scottish woman with a dry humour and an incredible style with patients, remarked that the staff's private beliefs outside Broadmoor are sometimes very interesting. She gave the example that some people who work at Broadmoor believe in the death penalty. Leeanne said that although everyone is of course entitled to their own views, she was not sure how someone could work at Broadmoor who really believes in the death penalty: 'You have to believe in hope,' she told us.

Staff, of course, experience their own form of admissions too. Jimmy Noak is now deputy director of nursing/clinical lead for quality improvement, Broadmoor Hospital, West London NHS Trust. He recalls just a three-hour induction on his first day in 1989.

Dr Gwen Adshead's recollection of her early experiences at Broadmoor was more negative when she described it to us. She was training as a forensic psychiatrist and so had to do some time at Broadmoor. Gwen found it very repressive and during induction the same big men in prison officer uniforms were patronising as they talked to the new recruits.

Her 'induction consisted of a talk which mainly was intended to scare us about how dangerous the patients were; how manipulative they would be; how we should never turn our backs on them and how they were cunning in the making of weapons. Much time was spent on showing all the weapons that the patients had made that were kept in Broadmoor's own version of the Black Museum at Scotland Yard. I also remember the speaker complaining about the ducks that landed in Broadmoor – really! – and how it was impossible to keep them out. There was very much an invitation to see oneself as stupid and naive if one attempted to see things from the patient's point of view. There was no sense that the patients were distressed or traumatised by their past, their mental disorders or what they had done.'

During a 2018 visit, it was explained to us that for staff, primary induction takes 12 to 15 days. Then they move on to supernumerary. Then there is a second induction on the ward. Generally, people have a month's induction then a three-month secondary induction, so it is far more thorough than it once was.

The key staff all work within an administrative building overlooking the hospital. The corridors and staircases are cramped, tired and claustrophobic. Any sense of 'them and us' is carefully avoided in this sense. The staff don't live in fabulous splendour or work in trendy open-plan workplaces. There is a whiff of the ward about many of their offices. What is surprising, though, is the cheery camaraderie. People are constantly greeting each other in hallways, popping their heads round the door during meetings and offering cups of tea.

Alex arrived at Broadmoor from prison at 24 years old. He was serving a life sentence in a dedicated prison unit for highly dangerous prisoners. They could no longer manage him in that unit.

In 2014, we met him on an admissions ward. He had been diagnosed with mental illness and personality disorder. One of the symptoms he was diagnosed with was 'auditory hallucinations'. Translation: he heard voices that weren't really there.

'I was doing a fruit salad for an assessment. I was cutting a mango with a sharp knife. The voices were tell-

ing me to attack the people in the room with a knife. They were goading me. I managed not to attack them. Two years ago, I would have done it.'

Alex was keen to progress from admissions. His medication had stabilised him and he wanted to move to assertive rehab, where he perceived that he would have far greater freedom.

There was a memorable conversation between Alex and a psychiatrist next to some bolted-down, plastic turquoise sofas. Alex claimed not to know when he would be moved. He immediately became very agitated.

Not everyone arrives in Broadmoor admissions by being directly violent. Some instead have exhibited highly disturbing behaviour which can cause grave risk to others. It was arson, for example, that led to Anthony's journey into Broadmoor.

Anthony's description of the mental illness which led to his fire-starting was truly extraordinary.

'When I was 19, I started eating large amounts of cannabis resin. I had a glimpse of things that I believed could solve the problems of the whole of the world and I became very grandiose. The total energy of the universe is God and you are God and I am God. I started doing bizarre things, like climbing on bridges and surfing on trains. In that period someone broke into my flat and kicked the door down and threatened me, and the door banged me in the face after I had been banging on the windows and I had been a nuisance neighbour and I didn't have a mobile phone, and after he left, I barricaded the door and set a fire and tried to get help.'

Initially sent to a medium secure unit after this peculiar incident, Anthony tried to start a fire there too. That act of arson directly led to him being sent to Broadmoor. He had been on preventative anti-psychotic medication and now at Broadmoor, his psychiatrist very much wanted him back on it.

Anthony did not want to take the medication. This reluctance to take medication is extremely common amongst Broadmoor patients and is very frequently encountered on admissions, especially amongst patients with long experience of heavy medication. Anthony, ever-articulate and unusually self-aware in comparison to his peer group, explained, with a haunting description, effectively being imprisoned within his own diseased mind.

'You feel absolutely terrible. You can't communicate. You can't do anything and it effectively makes me mentally disabled. My doctor is pointing out that the MOJ and probably the public will not accept me in the community off medication. Saying that, if I don't get medicated, I may never get out.'

As we saw time and time again, with patients like Anthony at the beginning of their journey, there is a long road ahead before they can aspire to assertive rehab, or ultimately, an exit from Broadmoor, back to a medium secure unit.

The history of the many people who have passed through the iconic main gate of Broadmoor and into admissions is on one level the history of our changing society over the last 150 years. We have all heard of Broadmoor's most notorious patients, past and present. What is less well known is how the type of people sent to Broadmoor Hospital has changed dramatically with the times.

Muslims now make up a significant portion of the Broadmoor patient population. In the 1980s there were a number of IRA patients. Does mental illness follow trends in society, or do societal trends drive the definition of mental illness? Practice development nurse Pat McKee noted that the age demographic has radically altered. Most admissions now are 'early to mid-twenties or thirties. There are lots more angry, young, violent men. Yes, there's an increase in jihadis now, but there used to be Irish terrorists in the seventies and eighties.'

Gwen Adshead posed a blunt, fascinating question in this context of religion at Broadmoor.

'We have the majority of patients having no religion at all, but some patients identify as Christians and then we have a steady trickle of people converting to Islam. As part, they would say, of turning over a new leaf. It is rare to have people from the Jewish faith and very rare to have anyone Chinese. They are not in prison either. There is a big UK Chinese community. Some of them must be mad. Some of them must be breaking the rules but they don't find their way into the system. It is a mystery.'

In other words, do certain ethnic groups or social strata suffer from mental illness far less than others, or are other factors at play in diagnosis and admissions decisions?

Statistically, black people are more likely to be diagnosed as schizophrenic or suffering from another psychotic illness, they are more likely to receive higher doses of medication and less likely to receive therapy, and they are more likely to be detailed in hospital under the Mental Health Act and to be detained on locked wards. It is tragically clear that work needs to be done urgently to address these inequalities.

Chapter 4

Intensive care

Between the two of us over the years, we paid a number of visits to the intensive care ward, including one together in 2018. It is hard to be prepared for a visit to Cranfield, the intensive care ward which houses the most acutely unwell patients within Broadmoor. Cranfield has 11 beds and, unlike the other wards, does not differentiate patients into mental illness and personality disorder.

Patients on Cranfield are either actively suicidal or pose an active high risk to others. Very often, it is both. The doors are kept locked and food is delivered through hatches. Quite often urine, semen and faeces are thrown from the hatch at the staff member as soon as the hatch is opened. Cranfield is a visceral place, where staff take their shifts on this ward one second at a time for their own safety and sanity.

What is termed 'eyesight observation' does exist in Broadmoor as well, of course, when patients are very unwell and dangerous. A number of patients, many suicidal or self-harming, have complained to us about this form of keeping watch, along with seclusion. Sitting outside the door of this claustro-phobic, sterile space is a nurse with their eyes trained on the secluded patient 24 hours a day in shifts. Not out of sight even for a moment.

On an intensive care ward which is called home by the most unwell patients in the hospital, the atmo-sphere is consistently tense. Electric, even. When a patient needs to be moved, the staff do the extraordi-nary 'six-person unlock', often wearing riot gear. We were privileged to witness a six-person unlock during our filming process. The door to the room can only be opened with six staff present.

On Cranfield Ward, every patient is subject to a long-term segregation agreement. This basically means that the patient is not allowed to mix with other patients on a long-term basis, because of the clinical risks that have been identified to be associ-ated with them mixing.

A nurse explained in Jonathan's film that 'There is a constant risk of violence on this ward. I tell them they are here because of violence and they will only progress from here if there is a reduction in violence. That is the message I give them.'

Consequently, the smallest things on Cranfield require a huge degree of risk and organisation. A patient wanting a drink of water, for instance. This utterly simple and basic human act requires the patient to back away from the door first. They then have to sit on the bed. Finally, the water is delivered through a small hatch.

On Cranfield intensive care ward, the men are always unpredictable and often violent. As with the drink of water, the simple act of serving a meal has to be carefully tailored to the individual. During a 2018 visit we saw the staff walking up to the hatches in the doors wearing latex gloves and looking through. Then they asked the patient to move and backed away from the door before it was opened a crack and food placed on the floor before the door was quickly slammed shut. It looked so humiliating as a ritual to us. Staff explained that on Cranfield, it was absolutely necessary.

With these most challenging patients housed on Cranfield Ward, violence is never far from the surface at all. During filming, we witnessed a patient refusing to return to his room from the yard. His primary nurse, Mo, had already given him an extra 30 minutes out there. Mo put on a camera to record the planned intervention in the event of violence.

The hospital forbade us from showing the restraint procedure on television. We had to replace the patient's voice with an actor's voice. Why? They argued that he didn't have capacity to consent. We offered to completely blur him to protect his identity. They still said no; they said this was not because they did not want us to show the restraint. Their objection was grounded in the fact that he did not have the capacity to consent. In the end, we compromised with an audio sequence set to a shot of an empty corridor.

There were eight staff members in total. They got him onto the floor and carried him to his room. There, he was restrained back on the floor and a final manoeuvre got him into his room somehow. Each staff member took a different role and held a different limb. The patient was placed on the bed, feet furthest from the door. A nurse held his head, another his legs, another his arms. They let go on exit, one by one. The last to let go in this highly choreographed situation is always holding his head and nearest to the door.

Whenever force has to be used, we know that staff take time out to discuss what has happened. It is stressful to witness, let alone to go through. Understandably, they need to talk it out.

Concerningly, a report in February 2017 showed Cranfield to be the most seriously understaffed ward in Broadmoor, with 1,303 actual staff hours as opposed to 1,808 planned staff hours. Occasionally, the hospital will pursue criminal charges against a patient following a staff assault, if the severity of the attack on the staff member merits legal action.

When asked how often violent incidents happen on Cranfield Ward, one nurse told us: 'Every other day. There are days when the ward will be very settled and the patients will be in a happy mood but not all the time because their mental state tends to subside a lot.' During the course of filming the TV show, Clinical Nurse Manager Ken Wakatama pointed out: 'Our focus when working with these guys is actually telling them that they are here not because of the illness, they are here because of the violence and they will only progress from here if there is a reduction in that violence.'

In one of our 2018 research visits for this book, Jimmy Noak had praised Ken Wakatama as an outstanding clinical nurse specialist, 'one of the most compassionate individuals', who of course worked closely with Jimmy.

Despite the threat level to staff, there is controversy over the use of physical restraint. In 1984, Michael Martin died in Broadmoor while being physically restrained. Joseph Watts died in 1988. Three years later, Orville Blackwood died after being forcibly injected with tranquilising drugs during a struggle with staff that began after he attempted to punch a doctor. All three of these men were black. In 1993, a report called 'Big, Black and Dangerous' was put out by the Committee of Inquiry into the deaths of Martin, Watts and Blackwood, who had all died in seclusion cells at Broadmoor. The report made a number of recommendations in addition to recognising the specific problems facing black mental health service users. Many of the recommendations centred around drug therapy.

Violence Reduction Specialist Pete Turner talked about deaths in custody when we spoke to him for our book interview and mentioned Orville Blackwood. As Pete pointed out, in the early eighties there was no formalised training for control and restraint: 'Neck lock, sweep, rugby tackle.' That was it.

Blackwood died at Broadmoor in 1991 after being injected with powerful anti-psychotic medication. The West Berkshire coroner, Charles Hoile, defended the doctor who injected Blackwood, refuting the idea that he could have criticism levelled at him or that he had acted unprofessionally.

The inquest reached a verdict of accidental death, but Blackwood's devastated mother said after the hearing:

'I am really disappointed at this verdict because my son has died at the hands of so-called capable staff in Broadmoor and it seems no one has accounted for it. The appalling thing is, this is the third young black man who has died in Broadmoor in the same circumstances and this is accidental death. I can't understand it.'

The other two deaths she referenced were Michael Martin and Joseph Watts. Like Blackwood, Martin and Watts had been diagnosed with schizophrenia and had died during their stay in Broadmoor after being restrained and injected with drugs.

When Broadmoor got an inadequate Care Quality Commission rating in 2015, one of the criticisms levelled was its high level of face-down restraints, a potentially dangerous practice that the government was trying to cut down. The obvious worry is that it can lead to asphyxiation. According to the CQC, about 30 patients a month were being physically restrained. Of these cases, 432 in total, 179 used the potentially dangerous 'prone position', in which the patient is trapped face down on the floor. Additionally, almost

three patients a month required 'rapid tranquilisa-
tion' to bring them under control. Broadmoor faces
the almost impossible task of showing appropriate
and restrained physicality to protect patients and
themselves, while at that time said patients may be
trying their utmost to do them physical harm.

Believe it or not, there some patients for whom even
intensive care is not a high enough level of supervision. Glenn Wright was sometimes described by
prison governors as the most difficult prisoner in
the UK. He presents a threat to himself and others.
After persuading two of his fellow cellmates to kill
themselves and being found guilty of their murder
and aiding suicide he was sent to Broadmoor in
November 2000. As a patient in a number of different high security hospitals in prisons he presented
with behaviours that staff found difficult to manage.
He would eat batteries to harm himself. He swal-
lowed razor blades and screws, and once put a razor
blade inside his foreskin. He pushed taps and broken
porcelain into his rectum.

Aside from being a threat to himself and to other
patients, Wright was a threat to staff. He threatened
staff, telling a prison psychiatrist that he would like

to kill her, slice her, fry her and eat her. He went through a period of keeping a cup of blood in his cell to throw at anybody who came close. For these reasons he was put into seclusion in intensive care. Here, he covered himself with faeces. Glenn Wright was in Broadmoor for just four months before doctors concluded he could not be safely managed in their facilities. That decision having been made, in March 2001, he was moved out of Broadmoor and spent the next year being shunted around frequently from one high security unit to another.

Forensic psychotherapist Gwen Adshead has a personal connection to a patient in Broadmoor. In the early 1970s, Gwen's father was friends with Derek and Jean Robinson, a York-based doctor and charity worker. Her father encouraged her to meet them for coffee since she was at university in York and they had a nice chat. Over 30 years later, she was shocked to hear that they had been murdered by Daniel Gonzalez, who suffered from a psychopathic personality disorder.

Gonzalez was sent to Broadmoor for the murders in 2006. He attacked six people in 48 hours, killing four of them. He is thought to have broken into the

Robinsons' house early in the morning – they had moved to Highgate, North London by this time – and stabbed them both to death in the hallway. It was a pointless, motiveless, random killing, although he told police of his desire to 'become Britain's most prolific serial killer'.

Gwen has 'always been interested in how other people's minds work. I was an internalist – on the spectrum I was towards the introspective end. If you are interested in how the mind goes awry and how organisations should respond, then you are going to gravitate to a place like Broadmoor.' She described the patients as 'our people' and 'not mad or bad but sad'. She quotes Shakespeare's phrase from *King Lear* – "ruined pieces of nature". I imagined these men as the beautiful babies they must have been – or as round-headed eight-year-olds. All that promise … how sad it is,' she said.

She never got a chance to help Gonzalez, the Robinsons' killer, despite working in the hospital where he was sent. Once he arrived at Broadmoor, he set about attacking his seventh victim – himself. He attempted suicide by opening the veins in his wrists with his teeth. One psychiatrist said he had never seen anyone bite himself with such ferocity.

He was placed on heavy doses of anti-psychotic and tranquilising drugs and put on four stone in weight in a year – it's a side effect of the drugs. But he never lost his desire for self-destruction. Three years after his admission, Gonzalez finally succeeded in ending his life, slashing his wrists with the plastic edge of a CD case.

The incident at the beginning of this book involves people who are no longer at Broadmoor, but whose lives underscore how difficult it is to rehabilitate those who truly are criminally insane. David Cheeseman renamed himself David Lant after his discharge from Broadmoor and made headlines again in 2004 after a sexual assault on a teenage girl during day release from a Norfolk prison. But of the two, it's Robert Maudsley whose notoriety has continued, both for the killing spree which took place after he moved on from Broadmoor to Wakefield and for his dubious and disturbing distinction of being the longest-serving British prisoner in solitary confinement.

No other British prisoner has experienced the same level of isolation for so long. The Moors Murderer Ian Brady had spent 51 years in prison after his 1966 conviction when he died. Brady met the medical director of Broadmoor but served his life sentence in another high secure facility, Ashworth. Since his death, Maudsley has taken the title.

Although there is much about Maudsley's story which is unique, the genesis of his suffering and the horrific suffering he has caused is grimly familiar. After a grotesquely abusive childhood, he developed a drug habit and became a rent boy to pay for the gear. His first kill was John Farrell, who had picked him up for sex. For some reason, Farrell thought it was a good idea to show Maudsley pictures of some children he had abused. Maudsley, no doubt reminded of his horribly traumatic upbringing, saw red and garroted him.

He was recognised to be mentally ill, declared unfit to stand trial, and after a manslaughter conviction, on the grounds of diminished responsibility, was sent to Broadmoor. There, he committed the gruesome murder which opened this book. Following that crime, he was deemed fit to stand trial, so this time the manslaughter conviction landed him in Wakefield Prison.

Unfortunately, Maudsley went on another killing spree. He lured Salney Darnwood, who had murdered his wife, into his cell and slit his throat with a knife made from a soup spoon, before shoving the corpse under his bed. He then spent a few hours trying to lure other patients into his cell but unsurprisingly, no one was up for it.

Maudsley's solution was to creep into prisoner Bill Roberts' cell and attack him as he lay in bed, braining him with a homemade knife and smashing his skull against the wall. It was then alleged that he ate some of Roberts' brain but Maudsley has always denied this. He then calmly carried the murder weapon into a prison office and let the guards know that they would be two short at the roll-call.

This activity led to a double murder conviction, but the baffling decision was made to keep Maudsley at Wakefield Prison. Considered totally unsafe to mix with other prisoners, he was placed in the solitary confinement that he has remained in ever since, and seems likely to remain in until his death.

He spends all but one hour of every day in 'the cage', a bespoke glass cell made for him in 1983 and which inevitably brings to mind Hannibal Lecter's cell in *The Silence of the Lambs*. Guards pass him his meals and other items through a small slot. Six prison officers go with him when he is allowed his one hour of yard exercise. He is forbidden from interacting with any other prisoners during this time. In the cage, he is under constant surveillance.

What are we to make of the cases of Glenn Wright, Daniel Gonzalez and Robert Maudsley? These are men who pose a deeply serious threat to themselves and others. During his last murder trial in 1979, the court heard that during his violent rages Robert Maudsley believed his victims were his parents. Born in 1953, the youngest of four siblings, all four of them ended up in care due to neglect. Shockingly, Maudsley's parents went on to have eight more children, and then were somehow permitted to take their eldest four home again.

Later, Maudsley was to say that all he remembered of his childhood were the beatings: fists, sticks, rods, a rifle. They were all used to brutalise him by the people he should have trusted the most. Social services removed him eventually and he went into foster homes. Drugs and suicide attempts landed him on psychiatric wards, where he often heard voices in his head, telling him to kill his parents.

His killings, his lawyers argued, were the result of aggression resulting from a childhood of near-constant abuse. Maudsley said: 'When I kill, I think I have my parents in mind … If I had killed my parents in 1970, none of these people need have died. If I had killed them, then I would be walking around as a free man without a care in the world.'

What, then, should we do for people like Robert Maudsley, whose upbringing caused this unfathomable damage? People like Maudsley, who were let down by social services when they were children but then went on to commit unimaginable acts of horror?

As former clinical director Dr Amlan Basu explained to us, 'Patients who come here will have perpetrated often horrendous crimes, and it's very easy to see somebody as either the perpetrator or the victim. It is much more difficult to hold the reality in your head that somebody might be both.'

Most of the time, a whole mix of early deprivation, poor education, family dysfunction and substance abuse feeds in. Amlan does not find it surprising that Broadmoor's patients tend to have mental illness and personality disorders.

'Everyone is born with certain temperaments and certain predispositions to certain behaviour, and if you've been given a whammy of genes, environment, upbringing, childhood adversity, substance misuse, then you develop a mental disorder. You do something that is horrific in whatever way you look at it. To then label that person as evil, I think, is a slightly kind of unthinking label.'

There has to be a belief in cure, though: 'It is a long-term project of putting someone back together and making sure they stay in that recovered state.' This belief was at the core of Amlan Basu's agenda in Broadmoor and his achievements there: 'One of the biggest misconceptions, I think, is that those who have severe mental illnesses or those who end up in a place like Broadmoor are destined to be unwell forever or to be risky forever and this simply isn't true. Mental disorders that we treat are very amenable to treatment.'

In Dr Gwen Adshead's view, even if it doesn't ultimately work, killers like Gonzalez must be helped to try. As a consultant forensic psychotherapist – a rare combination – she has spent her working life in the company of men at Broadmoor whom others would dismiss with a single word: evil. Her aim has always been to make them safer. Safe enough, ultimately, to be released from Britain's highest security institution for mentally disordered offenders.

'My job is to help a man become more articulate about what he has done, about his illness and about why that might be important for his future. Even if a cure is not possible, recovery of some identity is possible. My work involves talking to them and getting them to become more self-reflective. Violence is more likely to occur when people are not thinking straight.'

Chapter 5

High dependency wards

The high dependency wards are for patients who pose less of an immediate risk to themselves and others than those on Cranfield, but who are not well enough to be considered for the assertive rehabilitation wards. The mental illness high dependency wards are Ascot Ward, with 12 beds, and Woburn Ward, with 15 beds. The personality disorder high dependency ward is Epsom Ward, with 12 beds. For patients assessed at a slightly lower risk level, there is one medium dependency personality disorder ward: Chepstow Ward, also with 12 beds.

The high dependency wards have an unsettling atmosphere. There is a great deal of shouting, stress, locked doors and violence. The violence is often patient against patient; assaults on staff are virtually daily occurrences on these wards.

From the very beginning, we were keen to talk to the staff and patients about what it is like to experience one of these high dependency wards. Again, what we saw here were men who were raised in the most damaging of circumstances. Many parents feel guilty for what are – in comparison – mundane reasons: forgetting a piece of fruit for their child's lunch box, fretting over the amount of screen time they have. Many mums and dads worry that these small lapses in perfect parenting will have a detrimental impact on their child's future life. What, then, of children subjected to horrific physical, mental and sexual abuse?

Anile Parrymore, a nurse on Chepstow, made some very memorable patient observations from his long nursing experience in a secure hospital during the filming of the television series. 'I can definitely empathise with them. Often, they haven't come from different backgrounds to me, but they have come from different parents. You can probably see, if you go back into the lives of our patients, you can probably identify them at five or six years old. And say I'll be seeing you later on.' It is nothing short of chilling that Anile's experience created such conviction in him that the fate of many of Broadmoor's patients was fixed from early childhood. Critically, theirs was a childhood not just of deprivation and economic hardship, but of abuse too.

Many of the men we met during the book research and filming had chaotic childhoods. Many have been the victims of sexual and physical abuse. Childhood experiences, often shocking and sickening beyond belief, seal the fate of many patients very early on. Dillon's story, even in this bleak context, was incredibly powerful. When we met him for the film, Dillon was aged 49 and it was his second time in Broadmoor, as a patient in high dependency. Driven by mental illness and need, he'd been a violent offender and an arsonist: 'I shudder at a lot of the things that I've done in life and the bad mistakes and opportunities that I've missed.'

He remembers his childhood as a living nightmare – 'I got born into a satanic family – very, very violent. In some cases it would have been better to have killed me than to have allowed me to have had this abominable life that I have had. My father, thankfully, he died a homeless alcoholic. He was the bone breaker – he would break my bones. I had to learn pain very quickly. My father raped and beat my mother very badly. In his twisted thinking, he could raise a demon from the dead by raping her in the way that he did. From the moment I was born she freaked out, saying I was evil, my eyes were evil, and that was it. She kept trying to kill me. She would keep me locked up in the attic, I wasn't allowed to talk to my brothers. My mother, she also liked the sexual abuse, she was adamant that every single avenue of my childhood would be destroyed and she done her best with that. I was very thin, I had to steal my food, and it was fire that got me away. By the time I was five or six, I had learnt to light a match on the wall, like my mother did to light the gas oven. I was allowed to go to Kindergarten and I smelt the food, the boxes of sandwiches, and I scoffed my face big time and then set fire to the kitchen.'

Dillon later told us as a child he was tethered naked outside to a post and made to eat food off the floor like a dog, and sexually abused by his parents and their friends. He was in care from the age of seven to 18 and as an adult, he became a homeless alcoholic.

'I became an arsonist and a violent offender. Unfortunately, I did some kidnapping of some people who never did any harm to me. I was very very drunk. I threatened the police, I had the guns on me if I didn't put the knife down. I wanted them to kill me. I wanted them to kill that wild, out-of-control alcoholic inside me. And I was inviting them to do that. And I was very, very bloody close and then put the knife down.'

This is the type of childhood and adolescence, and subsequent substance abuse and psychotic behaviour, which can merit two stays in a Broadmoor high dependency ward.

The brilliant and dedicated director on the TV documentary, award-winning Olivia Lichtenstein, spoke to another memorable patient in high dependency through the tiny hatch of his door.

'I was a child soldier in Somalia,' he said. 'I had my first AK47 at the age of nine years old.' We were told that the patient was well on the way to moving to an assertive rehab ward and was doing really well, after this utterly shocking start in life on the other side of the world from Berkshire.

Dillon and the child soldier from Somalia are two extreme cases of childhood abuse that has brought both to incarceration in Broadmoor. Does evil exist in this world? Perhaps Dillon's parents, and the child soldier's captors were evil, but perhaps they had been abused as children in turn – Dillon's mother turned her own abuse towards her child – and their abusers had been abused, and so on. While it's true that many abused children do not turn into abusers themselves, it seems clear that a cocktail of factors, including abuse and mental illness, lead to the victims of abuse becoming violent criminal offenders in later life.

We observed Executive Director Leeanne McGee walking around the ward and talking to patients at the doors to their rooms. Trained as a nurse, she loves going back to the wards and being on the floor. 'It is where you want to be really,' she told us. 'It's better to spend the day with people that you are paid to look after than sitting at a desk, which can seem somewhat meaningless.'

In one crucial conversation about high dependency, Leeanne was keen to draw an important distinction: 'There is a difference between being mentally ill and not being mentally ill, and if you are mentally ill and have done something you are perhaps not in full control of at the time, society owes you a break and everyone deserves to have a bit of hope. If you have no hope, you are just going to give up.'

Having to deal with some of the notorious patients we have described, it is therefore no surprise that on the intensive care and high dependency wards, the job is incredibly demanding.

Broadmoor has 800 staff and many have been there for years despite the daily risk of assault. It may be a hospital but staff need specialist training from restraint, from giving patients forced medication to managing full-scale riots.

Staff members are carefully trained in the prevention and management of violence and aggression. Wearing helmets and shields, they are prepared for events that they are likely to encounter, including hostage and riot situations and armed patients. While this is highly unusual training for nursing staff, it is necessarily completely standard inside the walls of Broadmoor.

In the documentary, we attended breakfast time on Epsom, with the risk on Epsom Ward perceived to be a little lower than on other high dependency wards or, of course, Cranfield. We witnessed breakfast being pushed through the hatches. Patients on Epsom are allowed out to associate with each other, but only with plenty of staff around to watch. No room for complacency here, or anywhere within Broadmoor's walls.

An interesting story finally broke in the press about Epsom Ward in 2014, an incident several staff members had referenced to us in confidence. The incident was a riot at the hospital in July 2013, which NHS officials and the police had not put in the public domain, but which emerged as the result of Freedom of Information disclosures.

Patients managed to take over the nurses' office and were thought to have accessed confidential medical files on other patients. The police and an ambulance crew had to be called out to restore order. Thames Valley Police said they sent a 'public order response', also known as officers in riot gear, but that staff were able to get things back under control.

South Central Ambulance Service Trust sent out what they called a 'hazardous area response team' to Broadmoor and treated two people at the scene. The story only came out following an insider telling the *Health Service Journal* that staff shortage were so bad that patients were often locked in their rooms for 20 hours of the day. The CQC had already been told exactly the same thing about the staffing levels being too low.

The communications team at West London NHS Trust tried to deny that the riot had anything to do with Broadmoor being short-staffed. They tried to say that calling it a riot was exaggerated, and only two patients had got into the nurses' office and had managed to damage a ward. A Trust spokesperson wouldn't say how much damage or confirm (or deny!) the story about the medical notes being accessed, and they refused to release a report on security grounds.

It is salutary that as recently as a few years ago, during the time of Jonathan's TV show filming, this type of incident could take place on a secure ward. Even so, the majority of patients demonstrate enough healing and progress over time to transfer up to assertive rehab.

Chapter 6

The most notorious of them all

It's impossible to talk about Broadmoor and not talk about Ronnie Kray, the most famous high dependency inmate of them all. He is someone still almost obsessively alluded to by virtually everyone that we interviewed in the course of researching this book, such as Dr Gwen Adshead, who was on his ward, and his story, from the glamorous world of 1960s Swinging London to his death of a heart attack in Broadmoor in 1995, takes in what was also the most notorious period of Broadmoor's history: the 1980s.

Ronnie Kray and his twin brother Reginald must be the most infamous figures in the history of British gang crime. During the 1950s and 1960s their gang, The Firm, were the power behind much of the organised crime in the East End of London. Their nightclub circuit and celebrity network took in actors, singers, boxers, peers and politicians. The Krays associated with everyone from Judy Garland to Frank Sinatra. They were media savvy well before social media, working TV interviews and leaking juicy stories to the press.

An early warning sign of their life in violent crime was their poor record during National Service. Having been called up in 1952, they often deserted before getting collared and sent back to the army. Ronnie had punched a corporal in the face on his first day, and subsequently, while AWOL, the twins attacked a police corporal. This landed them with a jail stint at the Tower of London, of all places. They ended up with dishonourable discharges. Both violent and unpredictable, Ronnie was also starting to show signs of mental illness, with hunger strikes, abrupt, unprompted violent episodes and arson.

Ronnie was first diagnosed as a paranoid schizophrenic at the age of 22. It was when he ended up in a mental hospital for respite care during a three-year prison sentence he was serving for grievous bodily harm.

Ronnie Kray's rap sheet includes murder and vicious assaults. An early but notorious crime took place in 1954 when he used a cutlass to attack members of a rival Maltese gang. When a jewel thief broke a Kray gang member's nose in 1962, Ronnie's vicious retaliation was to brand him, causing partial sight loss.

The Krays believed their own hype, and acted like they were above the law. In 1966, Ronnie entered the Blind Beggar pub and shot George Cornell dead in front of dozens of witnesses. Such was the Krays' East End reign of terror, they knew noone would come forward readily to testify. Even so, by 1969, Ronnie and Reggie Kray were on trial at the Old Bailey for the murders of Jack 'The Hat' McVitie and George Cornell. Their 39-day trial, which caused a sensation, was then the longest and most expensive murder trial in English history. They were sentenced to life imprisonment with a minimum of 30 years to be served.

Medical reports during their Old Bailey trial revealed that Reggie Kray took Valium for anxiety. The conclusion of the reports' author, Dr Denis Leigh, on Ronnie, however, was that he had been suffering with schizophrenia for over 16 years. He was heavily dependent on medication to manage his condition.

Speculation over the source of Ronnie Kray's lifelong mental health issues ranges from infant diphtheria to a head injury sustained during a fight with Reggie, aged nine. Regardless of what separated the brothers' mental states, what is clear is that their mental states were what led to their physical separation. While the two were originally held in the same prison, in 1979, Ronnie was moved to Broadmoor. He was held in a standard assertive rehab ward. The brothers did not have a straightforward relationship. On the one hand, they enjoyed that twin cliché of an almost telepathic bond. Following his release from prison, Reggie was permitted to visit Ronnie in Broadmoor but the meetings would often pass in eerie silence.

There, Ronnie very much missed his brother. He also, though, seemed much happier, according to his friend and connection with the outside world, Maureen Flanagan. He took pleasure in simple things. Being able to decorate his room how he wanted, including, apparently, the addition of a gramophone and fancy curtains. Freedom to dress as he pleased, in sharp suits, monogrammed handkerchiefs and cufflinks. He was dapper and flashy in Broadmoor, with diamonds and gold jewellery.

Ronnie Kray's second wife Kate thought that his fondness for Broadmoor above all was grounded in something more poignant and personal. Ronnie understood that Broadmoor was good for his mental health and stability, and the right place for him to be.

Reggie Kray missed his brother so badly that his own mental health took a nosedive. He self-harmed, slicing himself with bits of a broken watch in a failed suicide attempt. In the end, Reggie was allowed regular visits to Broadmoor to visit Ronnie.

Reggie Kray might have been one of Ronnie's most regular visitors but he wasn't the only one. He was also visited by Richard Burton, Ronnie's wife, the actress Barbara Windsor and Debbie Harry, lead singer of the band Blondie.

Ronnie left Broadmoor on just one occasion: for his mother Violet's funeral in 1982. Violet was very close to Ronnie, in almost daily contact with him by phone, and had also been a frequent visitor to Broadmoor.

Even in Broadmoor the twins made a mint from their lucrative brand, selling the rights to their story and hawking memorabilia. Maureen Flanagan would bring Ronnie Kray creature comforts and gifts for his fellow patients. She would also sell stories about him to the national newspapers, which filtered back to the twins via their older brother Charlie, who was also effectively their agent. According to Maureen Flanagan, a Kray family friend who styled their mother's hair weekly, the twins hated the film, particularly scenes in which Violet swore.

In 1985, Ronnie married someone who had been writing to him in Broadmoor, Elaine Mildener. They got hitched in Broadmoor chapel. *The Sun* newspaper paid a cool £10,000 to have access to the wedding. He and Elaine divorced in 1989. Rates had gone up by the time Ronnie married Kate Howard in 1989. He scored £25,000 for the guest list, wedding photos and a short interview with the bride.

Our contributor Clive Bonnet is in a press picture of Ronnie Kray's wedding.

Pat McGrath, legendary superintendent of Broadmoor, recalled to his writer son Patrick that Ronnie's dodgy East End associates would visit and hand out hefty tips to patients. The staff then had to go around collecting all the wads of cash from the gutted and confused patients.

Many of our contributors have remarked on Ronnie Kray's celebrity presence. Pete Turner, Head of Violence Reduction, recalled that 'Ronnie Kray would stand rigidly and say hello to frighten new recruits.'

When Dr Gwen Adshead started at Broadmoor as a trainee psychiatrist she remembers that she worked on a ward with Ronnie Kray. He was on the same ward as Yorkshire Ripper, Peter Sutcliffe, at this time: Henley Ward. Gwen explained that at that time there was a lot of discussion about whether to put all the high-profile guys in one place or to scatter them about the hospital and it was decided to keep them all together and the ward was staffed by quite tough men.

Gwen described how institutionalised Ronnie Kray had become when she first met him: 'Your identity, who you were, is taken away and you are given a new identity, which is to be a patient in Broadmoor and so you become men who do as they are told at least on the surface and they spend a lot of time working out who is important and who is not. Mr Kray was superficially charming, he had an East End charm. All eyes were on him and he knew it.'

It would be easy to regard Ronnie Kray's life in Broadmoor with the same sensationalist hysteria that greets descriptions of his life as a gangster. The truth is more complicated. While Ronnie did maintain a figure in the press that portrayed him as an eccentric and successful criminal, his time in Broadmoor was affected by periods of really bad mental health, with visits to more high secure wards such as Abingdon. In one particular incident, it was reported that he was assaulted and thrown against a wall by Peter Sutcliffe.

Sutcliffe wasn't the only infamous inmate Ronnie interacted with. He reportedly became good friends with Charles Bronson, who he had known from their stint together in Parkhurst in 1976. After Bronson's attempt to kill another prisoner failed because the tie he was attempting to strangle him with snapped, Ronnie attempted to cheer him up by arranging a visit from boxer Terry Downes.

When speaking about Ronnie over a decade after his death, Bronson said that their friendship was based on what they had in common – they were in Broadmoor and certified insane. They related to each other, their illness, their medication, their incarceration, and had a deep bond of empathy.

Bronson reportedly gave many of his artistic pieces to Ronnie Kray as presents. In a letter to Kate Kray, written in 2014 after a fight with prison officers, he said, 'I swear I see Ron's face. I know the mind plays games in moments of mad events but it is still a comforting thought Ron's still around. Made me feel happy.'

The Sun brought out a piece during the media frenzy surrounding Jonathan's two-part primetime documentary. It quoted a letter that Bronson sent to a pen pal about Ronnie Kray's stash of cigarettes and food: *'It was like a f*****g corner shop. Ronnie was living the life of a lord. I'd never seen nothing like it. I'd* *just had a load of years in prison with nothing. All of a sudden I'm sitting there and eating tins of salmon.'*

Ronnie Kray made use of the art therapies in Broadmoor, and was especially fond of painting. He missed his twin brother and wife and in that sense wanted to leave but also knew it was the best place for him. First and foremost he was a Kray though, so he wanted to glamorise his time there and his own incredible gangster persona and myth-making too, though. Ronnie had a heart attack in Broadmoor and died two days later at Wexham Park Hospital, Slough on 17th March 1995. Reggie was allowed to attend his brother's funeral in handcuffs on prison leave.

Chapter 7

Rehabilitation

Assertive rehabilitation is the best option in the hospital for the most stable and least violent patients. It is also the recognised staging post before a patient is deemed fit to leave the hospital and move on to a lower security environment, or even the outside world. Broadmoor is undeniably a word that makes many people shiver. Yet as Jason, another patient we met on an assertive rehab ward, tells it, 'Broadmoor has got all this history of us being monsters but you can be violent and that doesn't make you a bad person because you might not have intended it.'

Assertive rehab houses by far the largest group of patients. Within mental illness services alone, there's Harrogate Ward, which has 20 beds with one bed for patients with physical healthcare needs, Leeds Ward and Sheffield Ward, each also with 20 beds, and the smaller Sandhurst Ward, with 12 beds. Then within personality disorder services there are three further large assertive rehabilitation wards, known colloquially within the hospital as the 'Kents': Canterbury

Ward, Dover Ward and Folkestone Ward, each of the three with 20 beds.

The contrasts between assertive rehab and the wards for the most unwell patients are striking. In assertive rehab, bedroom doors are left unlocked during the day. There is a communal space on the ward with a TV, albeit one behind a Perspex guard screen. There are newspapers, though they are screened for content. There is a kitchen where patients are permitted to make tea and coffee and to have biscuits. It feels faintly like a boarding school.

Assertive rehab includes Sandhurst Ward, for several decades the home of Yorkshire Ripper Peter Sutcliffe along with Kenneth Erskine, known as the Stockwell Strangler, and other extremely high-profile patients. A classic, low, Victorian T-shaped block, it has around 14 bedrooms. It enjoys a private garden at the end, where Sutcliffe once took regular exercise.

It is hard to get onto an assertive rehab ward, competitive in a way. For most patients it is an aspiration. The atmosphere is generally less tense, almost collegial. Talking to the patients there, it is evident that many of them are at a point in their recovery where they are examining their lives. What brought them to Broadmoor; what might get them out some day.

These wards are where each patient works towards being transferred to a place of lesser security. While many safety measures are still in place, such as the beds being bolted to the floor and activities stopping at 8pm each day for security checks to take place, there is a feeling of increased freedom. In this less stressful environment, patients are encouraged to take individual responsibility for their own care, which can include programmes away from the ward.

One of the most memorable characters that we met in Broadmoor, with a truly haunting story, Dante went straight to an assertive rehab ward. He was never assaultive or violent inside the hospital. Dante chose, tellingly, to rename himself inside Broadmoor from his original first name Jack. The name change is derived not from Dante Alghieri, medieval writer of *The Inferno*, but from the main character, Dante, in the *Devil May Cry* video game series.

We met him when he was 24. Aged 14, Dante killed his 11-year-old sister. In the same night, he attacked his 12-year-old brother with an axe, leaving him with serious head injuries, and set fire to his home in South London with his family inside. While his older sister and mother escaped the house, his younger sister died of smoke inhalation. Dante initially claimed he had been forced by a gunman to attack his sleeping brother and then set fire to the kitchen.

He was forced to admit this was a lie after incriminating evidence was found under his bed. There was a note that read 'Kill Family. Lose memory. Get adopted by rich couple. It all starts'. The note set out a deathlist, including his parents and three siblings, and the suggestion that he should cut himself to make it look as though a demon had committed the crime, not him.

Dante's trial included assessments from seven different psychiatrists, who could not agree on a diagnosis. The defence argued that he was autistic, suffered from mental illness, and had visions. The prosecution objected that he had excellent school reports and, until this point, his parents had noticed no behaviours that could possibly have warned them what he was capable of. Dr Paul Chesterman, the prosecution psychiatrist, conceded while in his expert view Dante did show psychopathic traits, a full assessment could not be undertaken until he was 18 years old.

Dante was found guilty of murder, attempted murder, and arson with intent to endanger life. He was convicted by a 10–2 majority at the Old Bailey in January 2006. Judge Richard Hone sentenced Dante to a minimum of 15 years, with two additional 15-year sentences for the attempted murder and arson, to be served concurrently.

To us, Dante came across as calm, eloquent, and a bit shy. He saw himself as a rather puzzling character. A phenomenally talented artist, he was working with graphite and charcoal to draw photo-realistic portraits of himself and people he knew from popular culture.

When we met him for the TV documentary he said, 'I've been a bit of a conundrum for the psychologist. I've had nine different diagnoses from 30 different doctors, I've had seminars about me done and people wanting to write books on me just because of the unusuality of my offence and my age.'

Dr Gwen Adshead said of Dante, 'He was ambivalent about whether he could get out or not. When you kill family members like that, it is very hard to live with. I don't want to underestimate the existential challenge of doing something terrible to people that you love. If you have killed someone that you love it is in your eye, your inner eye, the whole time. And you try and push it away and try and get on with reading the newspaper and working in the shop and going down to the gym but then you remember again and again and again. And I think it is intolerable.'

The idea of 'waking up', based upon Dante as an example, interests Gwen. She wonders whether many of the patients in Broadmoor have been in a 'form of dream'. Then there is a point at which they wake up to what they have done and the reality of what they have done and that now they are dead socially. They can never, ever go back to their old identity, they have killed themselves off. That identity is not going to come back: 'The only thing that is on offer is to be the man that killed his sister or whatever it is. And do you want to be that man? What does it take to be that man?'

Coming to terms with the reality not only of their crime, but of the impact it has on their identity and place within society is a profound and extraordinarily traumatic process. When speaking with Dante, he seemed to still be working with this concept, saying: 'I've probably never actually said the words of what I've done, I've never actually admitted it. I still get flashbacks. It's mainly guilt – I still struggle to bring it to mind, it's just a blur in my head. I've done such a terrible thing. One of things that I've got to come to terms with eventually is that I've done this, it's happened, and it will be with me forever.'

Dante said he felt 'lucky' that he never went to a high dependency ward but came straight to a rehab ward. He was, like the vast majority of his co-patients on assertive rehab, taking medication and undergoing psychological therapy.

An extraordinary part of Dante's case was the ongoing support of his family. Despite the nature of his offence, they remained in contact. He said, 'My family are my saving grace, to be honest – they're hugely supportive. […] What a lot of people see is that once a family member has committed an offence against a family member then the family disowns them. But they told me they'd stay by me, and they have.'

An essential part of assertive rehab is the relative freedom that it affords patients. Patients on assertive rehab are often allowed to go shopping under supervision, and to work in its internal carpentry and arts and crafts workshops, for which they are paid £1 an hour. They also have more freedom to explore their hobbies and interests. Music therapy is another way for patients on assertive rehab to get downtime, gain confidence and distance themselves from their gruelling treatment programmes.

Dante too was able to develop his own particular skills. While young, he enjoyed video games. As a child, he assembled and painted Warhammer figures and his father had tried to get him interested in target shooting. He also, of course, engaged in artwork. While, at Dante's trial, these hobbies were all mentioned as factors that ostracised him at school; within Canterbury Ward they gave him the freedom to express himself. The walls of his room were covered with pictures he had done, lots of them taking their inspiration from Warhammer. He showed us portraits he had created in graphite and charcoal of celebrities, and, disturbingly, a self-portrait with 'XIV' tattooed on the neck, indicating the age at which he committed his offence.

About the importance of this, Dante said: 'They've always agreed I have Asperger's. One of the problems I have is that I'm not very good at understanding emotions, or I'm feeling something I don't always understand what it is that I'm feeling. But if I can draw it, I can get out these angry feelings or these frustrations of being locked up, or guilt or remorse, and all these negative feelings I can channel through this imaginative artwork.'

But Dante's outcome is not a happy one. On 1st April 2015, he took his own life. Unable to cope with the guilt associated with his act of extreme lethal violence, he overdosed on anti-psychotic medication, 11 years into his 15-year sentence.

The last entry in Dante's journal read:

'I know what I am going to do. It won't be easy, not for those who cared.

'Please look after my family, they will not understand. No point in dragging this out any longer, hell's jaws await me. Death is awe.'

An inquest was held into Dante's death, which ruled that he had deliberately taken enough medication to kill himself. Dante's parents, Donald and Barbara, attended. Ms Ruvenko Sakupwanya, Dante's primary nurse, told jurors how, in the days prior to his death, Dante had twice asked to visit the hospital chaplain, and that, as the anniversary of his sister's death approached, he had been struggling with insomnia, depression and anxiety, as well as being treated for epilepsy and bipolar disorder.

Several staff members who worked closely with Dante emphasised to us in conversation the deeply vulnerable moment when, through medication, therapy and healing, a patient begins to have full consciousness of the crime that brought them to the hospital in the first place. It is a point of profound fragility which proved lethal in Dante's case.

If patients do well in high dependency, they get to move to the greater freedom of an assertive rehab ward. They have keys for their rooms on these wards. When we met Adam, for the TV programme, he had been on Canterbury Ward for the last four years. Before that he had been on a high dependency ward for nine years.

Adam showed us his room. He complained to us that the room was small, about six foot by three foot. However, it was larger than that. He strongly objected to the adjoining toilet, too. As he remarked plaintively, 'The only problem with having the toilet in there is that we also have our wardrobe in there.'

Convicted of arson, Adam was serving a life sentence in prison. In prison, his self-harm became so acute that he was moved to Broadmoor. His description of the abuse and subsequent self-harm that led to his Broadmoor admission is nothing short of nightmarish.

'I had a long history of self-harm and when I was in the prison service it escalated to the point that I was putting my life on the line on a daily basis. I was cutting tendons. My hand is on backwards as I have a wound here where I cut all the tendons and all that. I had a very traumatic childhood. My parents didn't love me the way they should of. I was sexually abused by several people outside of the family and because of the sexual abuse I started self-harming from the age of eight years old. I started by pulling off my toenails and setting fires. I grew up hating everyone, hating society and hating life. Self-harm was a way of me escaping all of that.'

Adam's Broadmoor journey was long, with many setbacks, but the end appeared in sight for him. He was allowed out to a medium secure unit, 30 miles away.

Assertive rehabilitation has also, unfortunately, played host to some notorious suicides. We have already seen Dante's death; Mohammed Omar was another such case. He was found hanging by a tie from the bars of his window on Folkestone Ward, with his hands tied behind his back, in 2005. He had used his bed to block the spyhole to his room. Suspecting possible foul play, as the staff wondered if another patient had bound Omar's hands behind his back, the police were called in.

Omar had started out by serving a life sentence after conviction for a 1991 murder. He was a paranoid schizophrenic who harboured the delusion that he was God. A political asylum seeker from Somalia, Omar came to Broadmoor in July 1992 after a murder in Stockwell, South London. Starting in a very high security environment, he had gradually moved through high dependency to the lower risk ward of Folkestone. He had been refusing medication. Low-risk patients were routinely checked on once an hour, partly to mitigate the risk of suicide. However, Omar was in the old part of the hospital, which hindered the effectiveness of some 'ligature point' checks. A ligature point is any feature in the hospital which could be used to fashion a strangulation device, usually a form of noose, creating a suicide risk for patients. Unfortunately, given many patients' ingenuity in the field of self-harm, ligature points are challenging to identify, at least to the point where all risk is eliminated.

On a lower risk ward he had access to items he wouldn't in higher security – belts, shoelaces and, of course, ties. A knots expert, Geoffrey Budworth, investigated and made a statement read out at the inquest. It said that one wrist was tied up very tightly but one was very loose, suggesting Omar had attempted to tie them himself. This was an important part in leading to the police conclusion that no one else was involved in his death, and the closure of the police investigation.

Hospital services director Maggie Gerdner was quoted saying of these ligature points: 'This is an ongoing issue with the old buildings at the hospital. They are Victorian and they have bars on the windows. The bars have been identified as a risk previously. In the high dependency areas a lot of work has been done to remove ligature points. This is obviously harder in the old Victorian buildings. It's a funding issue. We have put forward a new policy to the government but it's an ongoing problem.'

This case raises many interesting issues about Broadmoor in 2005, and it is clear that much has changed for the better since then. This sense of the older buildings not being fit for purpose fed very actively into the ongoing construction of the new hospital. Politicised discussions around funding, or lack of it, obviously remained as lively a topic as they had been in the 1980s and 1990s. The reference to Mohammed Omar refusing medication is intriguing too. A common theme and one in this case that seemed to go hand in hand with elusive and secretive behaviour, including not disclosing any suicidal thoughts.

Given that patients can display such ingenuity in self-harm, and that Omar previously attacked a staff member on a higher security unit, this is a case in point about why security is never far from anyone's minds at Broadmoor.

Chapter 8

After rehab

I t is possible, however, for even the worst offenders to be rehabilitated, even if it doesn't mean being released into the world. But what does it mean to rehabilitate a criminally insane mental patient? What should we do with patients once they have responded successfully to treatment? Should they still be punished if they were judged to have no control over their actions? And what does that mean for the families of their victims?

One example of this is Peter Sutcliffe, who gained the nickname the 'Yorkshire Ripper' and is one of the most notorious serial killers in English history. In 1981, he was convicted of murdering 13 women and attempting to murder seven others. He spent a large chunk of his long Broadmoor stay in Sandhurst Ward, an assertive rehab ward.

The women that he murdered were Jacqueline Hill, Marguerite Walls, Helen Rytka, Barbara Leach, Yvonne Pearson, Patricia Atkinson, Emily Jackson, Wilma McCann, Irene Richardson, Josephine Whitaker, Jean Jordan, Jayne MacDonald and Vera

Millward. Their ages ranged between late teens and early forties. Sutcliffe smashed in his victims' skulls with a hammer before stabbing them with knives and screwdrivers.

His attacks on women began in 1969, with murders taking place between 1975 and 1980, before his arrest in 1981 put an end to the unspeakable horror. Sutcliffe, a lorry driver and former gravedigger, reported that he had made the attacks after being told to do so by the voice of God. Despite being refused diminished responsibility at his trial, he was diagnosed with paranoid schizophrenia and later transferred to Broadmoor in 1984. His stay would last 32 years and cost the tax-payer in the region of £10million.

He was allowed out only twice: to visit the place where his father's ashes were scattered, and to be treated in Frimley Park Hospital, Surrey, after an attack which blinded him. Both times he was accompanied by at least four staff.

In March 1997, Ian Kay, a robber and murderer, attacked Sutcliffe with a pen, stabbing him in both eyes. This blinded his left eye and severely impaired vision in his other eye. Kay had not shown any previous hostility to Sutcliffe, and Broadmoor staff are highly alert to any issues and personality clashes between patients which can lead to violence. Staff had taken a razor blade off Kay but he'd claimed it was intended for self-harm rather than violence against others. It was suspected that he had been trying to make a name for himself and increase his stature by carrying out the attack. The Yorkshire Ripper was quite a 'scalp' for anyone that way inclined.

A decade later, paranoid schizophrenic Patrick Sureda, who had murdered his mum, attacked Sutcliffe with a knife. Around 20 patients witnessed the attack, during which Sureda yelled at Sutcliffe for being a rapist and murderer and expressed a keen interest in blinding his remaining 'good' eye. Following the attack, it came out that Sureda had been letting other patients know he planned to blind Sutcliffe. He was pulled off Sutcliffe by nurses before he succeeded.

While inside Broadmoor Sutcliffe remained the subject of intense media attention, to the extent that it became a threat to Broadmoor's security. A *News of the World* photographer took unauthorised pictures inside the visitors' centre. His ex-wife was papped when she went to visit him. The news of the Sureda attack on Sutcliffe came out suspiciously fast, being published by *The Sun* less than 48 hours later. It was obviously leaked or procured by some dodgy means, as Kevin Murray, then clinical director, pointed out.

There have even been cases of journalists going undercover and trying to gain employment at Broadmoor in an attempt to get close to patients like Sutcliffe and secure scoops. Public interest is huge. The question of privacy meets the right to know: while journalists may regard themselves as attaining information in the public interest, they are interfering with the functions of a mental hospital.

The families of Sutcliffe's victims were understandably horrified and deeply upset by the press harassment and industry that had grown up around him in Broadmoor. Family members trying to visit Broadmoor patients were also harassed by the press and made to feel uncomfortable, and felt discouraged from paying visits. Broadmoor management were also worried that this ridiculous media circus was having a massive effect on the hospital's ability to operate effectively.

Sutcliffe received visitors, letters and fan mail from every corner of the globe. He had an allowance of four visitors a week, who after what sounds like a fairly cursory assessment would be allowed to stay for up to four hours. Dr Gwen Adshead vividly remembers a young Peter Sutcliffe being a patient at Broadmoor and recalls the incredible cult of celebrity around him back then.

'The hospital was regularly maddened by this steady stream of women who wanted to visit Mr Sutcliffe. And Mr Kray's family often wanted to come and visit. We had to manage the outside world. It was also a time when the staff would often sell information to reporters down the pub, which then caused no end of problems.

'We had no shortage of headlines from the red tops in this period. The hospital in the eighties was subject to a kind of mad scrutiny. There was such a discrepancy between what the red tops were printing and the reality of working or living there.'

One of Sutcliffe's regular visitors was the TV personality Jimmy Savile. They enjoyed tea and a natter together. The mind boggles at what the content of those conversations might have been, and the sheer unbelievable weirdness of the whole scenario.

It was in the 1980s that a bizarre incident seems to have taken place which says a lot about both Savile's powers of manipulation and two strange and permeable aspects of Broadmoor appear to have been back then. Jimmy Savile arranged for Sutcliffe to meet former WBC Heavyweight Champion Frank Bruno. Savile ensured a photo was staged of Sutcliffe and Bruno shaking hands, with himself in the background, holding a cigar. Bruno said afterwards that he had no idea who he had been meeting, or that cameras were there to record it all.

Even before considering the controversies of his stay, the question is raised of how to begin treating a serial killer as notorious as Peter Sutcliffe. While schizophrenia can respond well to treatment from drugs and therapy, it cannot actually be cured. A person suffering from schizophrenia often cannot tell the difference between their own thoughts and reality, and as a result, their behaviour changes due to their illness. While Sutcliffe's claim of diminished responsibility due to these circumstances was rejected at his trial, it raises the possibility that, if the condition could be treated, managed, and brought under control, would the person still be a threat to society? And if they are no longer a threat to society, what should be done with them then?

Sutcliffe point-blank refused treatment until 1993. Even then, his attitude didn't change, he was just forced to take antipsychotics by the Mental Health

Commission. The upshot of this was that he had a much better relationship with therapy. He had cognitive behavioural therapy (CBT), talking therapies and healing workshops. He cooked for other patients, made elaborate pottery and painted rural scenes. He also converted to become a Jehovah's Witness.

Sutcliffe was undeniably responding to treatment. In 2006, Kevin Murray, the psychiatrist in charge of his care for more than 13 years and clinical director of Broadmoor as a whole, indicated in a report that his risk of reoffending was very low.

While patients at Broadmoor are not given a release date, if Sutcliffe was transferred from Broadmoor back into the mainstream prison system, his release might become a possibility as he was not on the list of what was then 35 people in the English prison system serving Whole Life Orders – meaning that they could never be released. Sutcliffe had 'only' received a judicial recommendation that he serve a minimum of 30 years in prison.

As Sutcliffe's mental condition continued to improve, there was mounting anxiety amongst both the victims' families and the general public. If Sutcliffe's mental health had recovered, exactly what reason was there to keep him inside the wall? Could he

be released? This became a far more distant pros-
pect when the High Court Judge Mr Justice Mitting
ruled in 2010 that Sutcliffe would serve a Whole Life
Order. Sutcliffe tried to appeal the decision but the
appeal was overruled.

It was the view of Lord Chief Justice, Lord Judge
that, 'The sheer abnormality of his actions themselves suggest some element of mental disorder.'

This is an interesting point. Does committing
a crime of this nature automatically imply mental
'disorder'? Does this therefore apply to all serial
killers? And how does the judge distinguish between
this and the sort of mental illness that allows for
diminished responsibility? As the years have passed,
fewer and fewer people are clinically judged to be
sufficiently mentally ill to be sent to Broadmoor,
or other high secure hospital facilities for the
insane. Behaving in an evil or bizarre way no longer
automatically labels criminals with the 'mad' tag.
Criminal acts accompanied by erratic or peculiar
behaviour are increasingly likely to lead to prison
rather than hospital.

The message of this ruling was crystal clear. Even
if Sutcliffe was ever seen as mentally well enough not
to need the profound clinical support that Broadmoor

offered, the nature of his crimes meant that he would be spending the rest of his life in prison.

On 11th August 2016, Sutcliffe was ruled mentally fit to be returned to be prison. This ruling led to his move to HM Prison Frankland in Durham. Sutcliffe himself regarded the move as 'political'. What is certainly true is that his transfer to a medium secure unit, setting aside whether he was cured or whether he was safe, would save taxpayers something to the tune of a quarter of a million quid a year.

There were press stories of Sutcliffe's cunning plan to secure freedom, exploiting what he had identified as a legal loophole – the fact that despite being insane he was still put on trial for the killings.

Kenneth Erskine was in Broadmoor at the same time as Peter Sutcliffe. His nickname, the Stockwell Strangler, reflected his preferred method of murdering seven elderly male and female victims during a horrific crime spree in 1986. Aged between 67 and 94, they were all murdered in their London homes, often in their beds. Most of them had also been sexually assaulted and robbed. Erskine had his own little serial killer trademarks, like turning all the photographs in the homes over or around. He also liked to cross his victims' arms and tuck them up in bed, as if they had died peacefully in their sleep.

Like many of the other patients at Broadmoor, Erskine had a bad start in life. Both his parents abandoned him while he was still just a child, and he bounced between special schools. Erskine was obviously severely unwell years before he received diagnosis or treatment. While on a school trip he tried to drown other children. He also tried to hang one of his brothers and offered him cannabis.

This was the trigger to him becoming home-less, a substance abuser, violent, and a burglar. He spent time in Feltham Young Offenders Institution for burglary. It was the fingerprints and mug shots from his burglary convictions that helped the police to identify him as the Stockwell Strangler. He was released from Feltham in 1982 against the advice of doctors, and at some point in the next four years transitioned into the criminally insane state that led him to strangle and sodomise at least seven old men and women, from a Polish war veteran to a tenants association chairwoman.

From his arrest onwards, Erskine had been show-ing many signs of mental illness. During questioning, he was evasive, perhaps delusional, suggesting that while he had burgled the pensioners, someone else must have crept in after him and killed them. A second shaky line of defence was his suggestion under pressure that he didn't remember killing anybody but perhaps he had forgotten or done so without realising. The abnormal behaviour persisted at his trial at the Old Bailey, including masturbating in court and being told off for falling asleep.

Erskine did not take the stand or speak at his trial, but the tapes of his interviews with the police were played. In them he described a female voice whispering to him from walls and doors, making him dizzy and forcing him to do things.

'It tries to think for me. It says it will kill me if it can get me. It blanks things from my mind. I can't fight it.'

In much the same way as Peter Sutcliffe, Kenneth Erskine was denied diminished responsibility despite his mental health and in 1988, at the age of 24, he was sentenced to life imprisonment with a recommended minimum term of 40 years. This ruling took place even though a psychiatrist concluded after many long hours of interviews with him that Erskine had a mental age of 11 and an inability to tell the difference between reality and his bizarre fantasy worlds.

However, he was subsequently found to have been suffering from a mental disorder within the meaning of the Mental Health Act 1983. That finding led to his admission to Broadmoor. He was there for almost 20 years before being moved to Thornford Park Hospital in Thatcham, Berkshire. Kenneth Erskine was still a Broadmoor patient at the time of Jonathan's filming but had left by the time we were researching the book.

As with the majority of other patients, while being treated at Broadmoor, Erskine was able to benefit from one-on-one psychological treatments as well as small rehabilitation groups. Having been diagnosed with chronic schizophrenia and personality disorder, he was treated through a combination of medication and therapy on an assertive rehab ward.

A different side to Erskine seemed to come to the fore in 1996. When Peter Sutcliffe was attacked by Paul Wilson on Henley Ward, Erskine was one of the two patients who stepped in. Wilson had popped round to Sutcliffe's room on the pretext of wanting to borrow a video but then proceeded to strangle Sutcliffe with the cord from his stereo headphones.

It was Erskine and another patient – James Devitt who alerted the staff and piled in to help, arguably saving Sutcliffe's life. It's hard to say whether Wilson was trying to make a name for himself and play the big man with the attack. His own explanation was that he hated sex offenders, and given that he was 'only' in Broadmoor for violent burglary, there might be something in that.

Perhaps the most significant event of Erskine's time in Broadmoor though was his appeal against his murder convictions. Dr Andrew Horne, consultant psychiatrist at Broadmoor Hospital and one of Erskine's doctors for 20 years, said that Erskine's schizophrenia would have diminished his responsibility for his actions 'to a massive degree'.

The decision was announced by the Lord Chief Justice, Lord Judge, and two other judges at the Court of Appeal in London that Erskine's conviction would be reduced to manslaughter on the grounds of diminished responsibility. Lord Judge is on record as saying: 'This is a straightforward case. It is overwhelmingly clear that, at the time when the appellant appeared at trial, there was unequivocal contemporaneous evidence that his mental responsibility for his actions at the time of the killing was substantially impaired.'

In 2016, Erskine was moved from Broadmoor to medium secure unit Thornford Park Hospital in

Berkshire. The movement of both Sutcliffe and Erskine to lower security institutions got a pretty nervous response from the local public, not surprising given what those two were known for. However, since their respective moves neither Erskine nor Sutcliffe has been reported to commit a crime, despite the lower levels of mental health observation possible in such institutions. This could be down to their advanced age or the care of the institutions that they have moved to. But it does seem to support the attitude that assertive rehabilitation is capable of taking some of the most infamous serial killers in British history and managing their mental illness to the point where they can live within the normal prison population without being a threat to themselves or others.

Someone who perhaps hasn't been rehabilitated is the legendary Broadmoor patient Charles Bronson. He has never actually murdered anybody but still managed to win the title of 'Britain's Most Violent Man'. At age 22, Bronson was convicted of armed robbery in 1974. Initially, he received a seven-year prison sentence. This was extended as a result of his violent attacks on guards and fellow inmates. When he was eventually released after 13 years in 1987, he tried to start a career as a bare-knuckle boxer. However, he soon landed up in prison for planning another robbery. During this custodial sentence he showed a penchant for hostage-taking on multiple occasions and ended up receiving a life sentence. During this life sentence, he has been held at Broadmoor, Ashworth and Rampton.

Throughout his stay at Broadmoor he staged a number of rooftop protests, during one of which he did £250,000 worth of damage. Bronson also went on a 18-day hunger strike, and attempted to kill another patient with a silk tie. He called Broadmoor a 'cesspit full of pain, misery and despair'. Despite this, he thrived on the art therapy in Broadmoor, as he is a very gifted writer, poet and as can be seen from our exclusive illustration, cartoonist.

Bronson's violence towards staff, however, continued, long after he was transferred away from Broadmoor. During one terrifying incident he took an educational officer hostage for 44 hours. It was this act of hostage-taking that earned him a life sentence. After Arsenal won the FA Cup, Bronson smeared himself in butter and attacked 12 prison officers who were in full riot gear.

Bronson's way with words and dark wit, as well as his outrageous escapades, were part of what endeared him to the British tabloids. He eventually left Broadmoor and moved to Wakefield Prison in West Yorkshire. He has changed his name to Charles Salvador. A self-declared fitness fanatic and a prolific writer, he has dedicated a book to exercising in confined spaces, and as a talented artist, his painted depictions of prison and hospital life have been publicly exhibited and won him many awards. After such long service, including stints at all of England's high secure mental hospitals, it is difficult to envisage Bronson ever adjusting to life in the outside world ... in the unlikely event that he is ever granted the opportunity.

Chapter 9

Lockdown

Broadmoor could not function for a single day without the rigid security procedures and secure spaces within it, which are taken with deadly seriousness. There are 900 staff at Broadmoor and 200 patients, and the staff really know their patients, to the extent that they can do so, they know the risks that they present.

Broadmoor has the security status of a Category B prison. A Category A prison houses male criminals who are perceived to pose the greatest threat to the police, public or national security, were they to escape. Category B prisons are either local prisons housing prisoners who came straight from a local court either on remand or having received a sentence, or training prisons with long-term and high security prisoners. Category C prisons are for those who cannot be trusted in the outside world but are unlikely to attempt an escape, and Category D are open prisons. Clearly, Broadmoor is none of the above but purely from a security status point of view it is characterised as Cat B.

The first line of defence, as we have seen, is the biometric tests, airport-style security scans and a physical search, or 'pat-down'. Once through these barriers, a central control room strictly monitors and controls all movement. This means that the head of security and his team will know exactly where every patient is, all the time.

Broadmoor has a secure perimeter (two fences, anti-climb measures, supported by over 300 cameras, with a fence that is alarmed around the entire perimeter). The inner perimeter is marked by a very high, very high-tech, and highly intimidating steel fence running inside the hospital's brick outer walls. At points all around the hospital grounds, access is controlled by a set of seemingly impenetrable electronic gates.

Movement around the hospital 'campus' is strictly controlled. At various times of the day, a series of gates are opened and manned to allow freer flow of patients as they go to work or to therapy sessions. This is known as 'supervised movement'. It is a sobering reminder of how rare it is for the men to walk from one place to another without having to stop for doors and gates to be unlocked and relocked behind them, and it gives the place the feeling of a ghost town.

One of the clever and invisible tricks that the hospital plays on patients is a solution to what they call 'non-compatibility'. Often a patient will brag or threaten violence towards a 'celebrity' patient. As we have seen, Peter Sutcliffe, the Yorkshire Ripper, was a particularly popular target as his assailants hoped they would gain points with their peers if they managed to inflict an assault. No matter what the patient has done in the outside world, it's vital that they are kept safe inside Broadmoor's walls.

To control these issues, Broadmoor changes the movement patterns. That way, they can make sure that the threatening patient simply never comes across, or is ever in the same room as the other patient. Movement is so strictly policed and choreographed that this is possible. This choreographed movement around the site is striking to witness through the control room in the security office. It is a seamless ballet grounded in science, vigilance and advanced psychology.

Humankind's capacity to form hierarchy seems to exist in every sphere and in every extremity, and Broadmoor is no exception. Child sex offenders and rapists are at the bottom of the pecking order, and certainly often regarded with revulsion and a sense of moral superiority by other murderers and violent offenders. It was only during our Broadmoor research that we discovered the institution was the birthplace of the word 'nonce'. NONCE is a Broadmoor phrase, an acronym for Not on Normal Concourse Exercise. It was used to refer to paedophiles and sex offenders who were Not on Normal Concourse Exercise. They were not allowed to exercise in the yard along with the other patients, but had to be kept separate because of the high likelihood of being attacked.

Patients are searched throughout the day and, when in their rooms, are checked every 15 minutes. The threat of violence hangs unspoken in the air and, all too often, is directed by patients against themselves. Self-harm is a very big issue amongst these men and a perpetual reminder that they are suffering from mental disorders.

As one patient told us, 'Broadmoor's got all this history about people being all these monsters. But you can be violent, that don't mean you're a bad person, because sometimes you're not intending it.' We met a patient who had attempted to cut his own throat four times. Prior to entry to Broadmoor while in prison, he had tried to hang himself and was only just resuscitated in time when discovered by warders.

The restricted items collection at Broadmoor is a potent snapshot of security threats. These items form a potted history of some of the more creative and savage assaults that have exploded within the hospital walls over the years. We were shown some of the weapons that have been confiscated. Much of what we saw is truly ingenious. We were shown spoons and forks that had been sharpened and turned into a weapon. The staff have to be vigilant with everyday items.

Then there was a CD case that was meticulously shaved into a lethal pointed blade. A slashing across the throat in 2005 with one of these items led to CDs being added to the banned items within the hospital.

Bonfire Night was abolished in the 1990s at Broadmoor, after a patient chose the exact moment under cover of the sound of fireworks to let a firework off in another patient's face. In other words, however ostensibly normalised, even festive, the atmosphere becomes, the threat of violence is ever present.

There are on average five physical assaults on staff members each week, including punching, kicking, throwing hot liquids, urine and faeces. Some are serious enough to warrant the hospital pursuing criminal charges, though Broadmoor has a much higher threshold on this than a regular prison or ordinary hospital environment. The throwing of faeces or urine, for instance, in the face of a staff member would likely get you charged in a more ordinary environment. In Broadmoor assaults are regarded quite kindly and with the understanding that violence is intrinsic to some of the medical conditions suffered by the patients. Therefore the attack has to be quite extreme and deliberate in order to lead to specific charges being brought.

In addition, non-physical assaults, including racial, sexist and verbal abuse, occur up to 30 times a week. In 2006, for example, there were 228 attacks across the year, 15 of which led to a staff member being taken to an A&E department. Teams wearing riot gear are deployed an average of 30 times a year in order to administer medication to out-of-control patients. Assaults on staff can become so common that staffing levels have to take them into account. Reports on Broadmoor's staffing levels often contain notes concerning employees signed off sick due to assaults or incidents. The level of stress in the environment takes an emotional toll.

Broadmoor staff nurse Lucia Johnson landed £21,500 in compensation after two attacks from patients in December 2002 and July 2003. The first attack saw Johnson enter a patient's room. The patient had a reputation for throwing things at staff, and this meant all his stuff was meant to be either removed or secured in his room somehow. It hadn't been, so he managed to injure her left hand and nose.

The second incident involved the same guy. He was trying to kill himself by strangling himself with ripped-up textiles so Johnson and three other staff members went into the room, leading to a struggle in which Johnson was repeatedly punched in the face and upper body, causing her to take months off work to recover from her injuries. The investigation found that the patient was known to be violent but there had not been enough measures taken to protect staff, despite this knowledge.

Dennis Sterling, a patient admitted to Broadmoor for violent and sexual crimes, was also a diagnosed schizophrenic. In January 2011, he sexually assaulted a female nurse in an attack so horrendous that she had to take long-term leave to recover. Judge Nicholas Ross said: 'This was an attack on a female member of staff. It was terrifying. That you continued to be sexually aroused after the attack is clear to me.'

While Sterling pleaded guilty to sexual assault, his defence lawyer, Jennifer Osborne, made an unusual request: that he be allowed to move from Broadmoor to a regular prison, stating the belief that he was less likely to be a threat to women there. Apparently, Sterling was aware that he posed a grave danger to women and he reckoned that with fewer female staff members in prison than at Broadmoor, he was better off there.

The judge turned down this request due to the nature of Sterling's mental illness requiring him to be treated in a psychiatric institution, which raises the question of whether this prioritises the health and safety of the inmates above those of the staff.

In 2015, there was a grim attack on two Broadmoor staff members, aged 63 and 54. Apparently, the incident kicked off when two patients, both recent converts to Islam, were told they could not pray in the day rooms or dining areas. The patients smashed up some DVD cases and a cup and used the sharp broken pieces to inflict horrible injuries, including facial damage. They also punched the staff members. Broadmoor did not disclose what the staff roles of the two men were, but they both required hospital treatment.

And of course, staff members are not the only people attacked in Broadmoor. In 2004, one patient, Peter Bryan, murdered another, Richard Loudwell, by strangling him with a trouser cord. Bryan had been in Broadmoor for just ten days, having been placed there after murdering his friend Brian Cherry with a hammer and beginning to cannibalise the corpse. Police had found him cooking his friend's brain in a frying pan.

The attack on Loudwell took place in the ward dining room. According to an official report into the incident, there were up to ten patients in the day area of the ward with no staff physically present. The nearest staff were in the ward office, where they could see into the dayroom but not the dining room. Bryan had hit Loudwell's head against the floor in addition to using the cord around his neck. He indicated to a nurse after the attack that he had also intended to eat Loudwell, given the opportunity.

Vigilance is critical. Broadmoor's patients can be very ingenious. Jerome Carroll was sent to Broadmoor after a devious and vicious assault on a prisoner. A paranoid schizophrenic with personality disorder, Caroll conducted a racially motivated attack on fellow inmate Abdi Hussain which almost killed him when they were in Elmley Prison on the Isle of Sheppey together.

Carroll was taunting Hussain for being a black man and a Muslim. Looking for trouble, Carroll bashed him on the head, stamped on him repeatedly and then almost strangled him with a bedsheet before other prisoners stepped in and saved his life. Carroll had previous convictions for violence. He was serving a three-year sentence for the wonderfully bizarre conviction 'harassment of cousins'.

A number of the patients we met were very lucid and personable. During one of our visits to Chepstow, the medium dependency ward, Lenny wanted to show us his artwork and tell us about himself. Lenny was wiry and slightly manic. He wore a checked shirt and blue jeans and found it hard to stay still. He had been in Broadmoor for seven years and it was his second time in the hospital.

'I was a victim of paedophilia for nine years under the Home Office. It started when I was five or six. Although I am also an offender. I threatened to kill a Section 12 consultant psychiatrist with a machete. But I am not guilty of raping myself. I was being tied up, raped against my will, alcohol shoved down my throat, pacified with all kinds of medicines that belonged to that person so that I would be pliable and agree to have sex, which I didn't want to do. For nine years I was in the system, seeing psychiatrists at the same time as being raped, and no one did a single thing to help me. I am angry at the people who did what they did to me.'

Lenny was not happy with life in Broadmoor and told us he was bringing a high court case against the hospital. He was outraged that £300,000 a year is spent on keeping each patient at Broadmoor. That is five times the cost of keeping someone in prison. As Deputy Director of Nursing Jimmy Noak told us, staff members at Broadmoor are always mindful of the victims of crimes, and their families. But no matter how expensive, or how gruesome the crime, if someone has committed a violent crime while suffering from a severe mental illness, they should be treated in hospital.

One of the most memorable experiences we had during our interviews with Lenny while filming was witnessing a forced injection. Lenny refused to take his anti-psychotic medication and staff surrounded him. Staff told us to leave the ward and they made us turn off the cameras. They said we could see him the following day.

The next day he told us that they twisted and turned him and took him to seclusion. They took down his trousers and pants and held him down and injected him.

A doctor, however, offered a different perspective on this type of extreme event. He informed us that one of the great battlegrounds in the hospital between staff and patients is the issue of medication. The doctor explained that one of the difficulties with psychotic disorders is that 'your experience of reality is different. And you might feel very strongly there is nothing wrong with you. So it can become very acrimonious.'

Inside Broadmoor, staff know patients well enough to get inside their heads and know what they are likely to do next. It is called Relational Security.

One patient, Simon, who we met during filming, firmly believed that the hospital was trying to poison him.

'There are several staff who smell when they try and hand me something. Can they use gloves?'

A nurse tried to explain that if it is food that the staff are not directly touching or preparing then no, the staff will not wear gloves.

In a group therapy the same patient – Simon – became extremely exercised: 'All they ever talk about is RSU, RSU, every single minute, hour, day, year in, year out.' The men, around ten in total, sit in a circle, with a psychologist chairing the conversation.

The way out of Broadmoor is a long and winding one and usually ends up in an RSU: a Regional Secure Unit. They exist up and down the country. The patient continued, 'and if you do go to an RSU, all that happens is that they threaten you that if you don't behave, you will be sent back to Broadmoor.' The other men in the group murmur with approval at this deeply frustrating aspect of being a Broadmoor patient.

Simon had been bouncing around the wards inside Broadmoor for several years by the time this group therapy was taking place. He explained what had happened on a recent occasion: 'I am going to abscond, I am going to abscond. It is starting to really piss me off. I went into an office, closed the door behind me, blocked it with filing cabinets and I just trashed the office. It felt good.'

It's rare, nowadays, that prisoners break out of Broadmoor. But in the seventies and eighties, and fuelled by salacious headlines from the tabloid press, Broadmoor's already notorious reputation was added to by a number of high-profile escapes. Broadmoor security has been designed to prevent an escape ever happening again.

Broadmoor conducts annual audits on standards of security and in recent years has attained the high scores of 99 per cent, 99 per cent and 97 per cent in this area. There are major incident exercises and training, and contingency planning with police and local authorities. They work closely with Thames Valley Police and local authority emergency planning groups.

The new security measures have paid off. On 20th January 2018, West London Mental Health proudly published 'Top results for Broadmoor Hospital in security audit': 'Broadmoor Hospital has achieved the highest possible rating in NHS England's 2017 annual security audit. The annual security audit has given Broadmoor a "green – substantial assurance" rating. The audit was carried out by staff from Rampton and Ashworth High Secure Hospitals in 2017.'

Staff at Broadmoor are pleased with the very high ratings they have received for security standards in their more recent annual audits. It is the result of extremely hard work over a long period of time.

Chapter 10

The fugitive

Broadmoor has had its fair share of escapes over the years. From 1940 to 1949, there were six escapes involving six patients. From 1950 to 1959, there were seven escapes involving nine patients. Between 1959 and 1965, there were three escapes involving four patients. This compared favourably with the escape rates of other institutions at the time, but at Broadmoor, one escape is too many.

These escapes mean that all has not been harmonious in the hospital's relationship with the village. Broadmoor's sirens are notorious. For many years the noise of the alarms, for regular drills and, more infrequently, but far more disturbingly, for escapes, is at the heart of the psychological impact that the hospital has had on Crowthorne. Prior to 1957, there were two escape warning sirens, one at Broadmoor and the other at Little Sandhurst. In 1957, a temporary siren installed in early 1954 was replaced by a more effective electronic siren, which was meant to give adequate warning within a two-mile radius of the hospital.

Subsequent tests showed that the Little Sandhurst area was still poorly served, and a second siren was installed in March, 1961, which sounded at the same time as the main siren at the hospital. Further tests showed that although audibility in the Little Sandhurst area was much improved, there were still districts where it was unsatisfactory, so a number of satellite sirens were installed at distances of three to four miles from the hospital.

These were at Camberley, Crowthorne, Finchampstead, Wokingham, Bagshot and Bracknell. This entailed connection to the electricity supply and to the main siren at Broadmoor. For a long time another really difficult problem was the sounding of an all-clear. The mid-sixties choice of siren, a 'bleep, bleep, bleep', was far too easily confused with the local fire service sirens.

The Superintendent of Broadmoor and the Chief Constable of Berkshire worked out a plan of co-operation between the hospital staff and the police which operates in the event of an escape. The BBC worked with the police and the hospital authorities, deciding whether information should be broadcast.

In the 1950s, an escape of an inmate who subsequently murdered 'the little girl on the bike' drew both Broadmoor and its notorious sirens into an unwelcome sharp focus. John Thomas Straffen was a serial killer who had murdered two children in Bath. His mugshot is truly haunting. His eyes, sunken and lifeless, gaze at the camera, almost corpse-like, in combination with his mouth hanging open and his hollow cheeks. Straffen was diagnosed as having the mental age of a young boy following a childhood illness, and his mugshot suggests an individual too mentally unwell to have responsibility or comprehension of his actions. In 1952, a judge ruled him unfit to stand trial and he was sent to Broadmoor. Like many before and after him, he dreamed of escape. Like far fewer, six months into his hospital stay, he achieved it. The mode of his escape was simply to jump over the wall and run.

It took four hours for him to be caught. The pursuit was undertaken by staff on pushbikes, an evocative image of quite how low-tech everything was at Broadmoor all those decades ago. During those four hours, a five-year-old girl, Linda Bowyer, was murdered. There is some controversy today about whether it was Straffen who murdered her, or if he was a convenient fall guy for someone close to her. Straffen had readily confessed to the two murders in Bath. However, when questioned by police following his arrest, he denied killing Linda. At this stage, however, news of her death had not been broken, and Straffen then seemed to fully implicate himself by describing her as the 'little girl on the bicycle'. Nevertheless, in 2001, solicitors wished to re-examine the case and conviction on the grounds that he had not been fit to stand trial. An investigative journalist, Bob Woffinden, discovered that some local witnesses had the timing of Straffen's recapture before the time of Linda's tragic murder. Linda also had injuries on her body that could not readily have been caused by Straffen, who had no fingernails. To some former Broadmoor workers we spoke to, the time frame of reporting the little girl's murder doesn't add up. Straffen's mental incapacity and his death means these loose ends are unlikely to ever be tied.

Nevertheless, it was Straffen's escape, and the belief that he was responsible for the murder that led to an outcry demanding a siren, which went up to the very highest levels of British government. Local residents of Crowthorne and its surroundings were justifiably vocal in their concerns about their safety. In addition to questions raised in Parliament, Prime Minister Winston Churchill also queried the decision for Straffen not to be sent back to Broadmoor again after the escape. Was he not considered mad any more after what certainly appeared to be another brutal child murder?

Clive Bonnet paints a vivid picture to us of historic responses to escapes. Local schools closed. 'They had very specific orders – you couldn't leave school until your parents picked you up.'

Clive couldn't be much closer to the action on this count. His dad was in the press photo of Straffen coming back to Broadmoor, as his father was one of the very men who brought him back in. Clive said, 'In 1952, when Straffen escaped, we had one wall and bars on the windows!'

Frank Mitchell – who Clive calls 'the mad axeman' – was a heavily tattooed Kray associate. He was also rather good-looking, with a penchant for wearing his shirts unbuttoned more than halfway down. More to the point, he was a serial escapee, managing the feat an astonishing three times from different venues. In 1957, he escaped from Rampton after very cunningly making makeshift but surprisingly effective keys from bedsprings. He found time to attack a man during this break-out. Once he had been caught, he boasted to his judge, 'there is not a lock that I can't undo.'

In 1958, he escaped from Broadmoor by making a dummy and leaving it in his bed. He used another one of his homemade keys to get out, plus a hacksaw to cut through the bars of his room, and clambered over two walls. He managed to stay missing for three days, during which he earned his nickname by threatening a terrified family with an axe.

Mitchell was subsequently moved to Dartmoor Prison, where the Krays carried out a bold plan to break him out of prison, mainly in order to embarrass the police and grandstand about their power and ingenuity. Unfortunately, once the Kray gang member who'd helped Mitchell to escape realised how volatile and uncontrollable he was, he decided the best option was to shoot him dead and dump his body at sea, a sticky end for the mad axeman.

Writer Patrick McGrath in his reminiscences of Broadmoor had described a man he anonymised as 'Denis', who was a family friend and spent time at their house. When Denis escaped, McGrath's mother left food out for him until he gave himself up. This story becomes significantly less charming with the postscript that McGrath found out in 2009 that 'Denis' had raped a child during his period at large.

That story pretty much encapsulates the impossible balance between rehabilitating a patient, making them well enough to move on from the hospital and on the other hand, keeping the public safe from a dangerous criminal. With hindsight, noone can disagree that the community building freedoms of village life came too soon, if he would ever have been ready for them. But danger is difficult to assess. For a patient to be afforded more freedoms within Broadmoor requires the stamp of approval from a number of trained medical professionals.

Richard Upcher was initially admitted to Broadmoor on 2nd June 1961, under a hospital order with an unlimited restriction on discharge, after conviction for burglary. By the time he made his escape, he had been rewarded for good behaviour by going into a block with plenty of freedom of movement. If a patient seemed to be rehabilitating, wasn't it fair enough for him to move to a lower security arrangement?

Upcher, a small and skinny man, escaped from the block on the night of 21st February using a wonderfully ingenious method. He hid himself in a hot plate under the serving hatch in the dining room after the other patients had left. Then he broke a pane of glass in a window of the dining room and squeezed through the bars. He proceeded to scale an inner and an outer security wall, helping himself along with various tools and devices. Taking a ladder from a locked shed, he piled up some rubble from a site where patients had been doing manual labour.

Upcher was sighted on top of the outer wall at about 10.45pm by a nurse who, realising that he could be with other patients, ran about 300 yards to the house of another nurse, who telephoned the hospital lodge immediately. When the two nurses returned to the wall, the patient had gone.

The whole of the night staff completed their duty. Back then, the night duty staff times were from 21:00 to 07:10 the following morning. Once the patient's absence had been discovered, the escape procedure worked pretty well. Not much time was spent on the necessary check to confirm a suspected absence before sounding the alarm. Dry weather and a north-easterly wind meant that the main siren at Broadmoor could be clearly heard in the immediate area of the hospital in these conditions when it sounded at 11:05.

It was about 9pm the following evening when Upcher gave himself up to troops stationed in the

Caesar's Camp area, less than two miles away from the hospital. In the course of his escape, he hadn't actually committed any criminal acts against people or even property.

Clive's description of the escape gripped us. As he tells it, 'When Upcher escaped, the siren was going, it was pouring with rain, and Dad was setting up to go to the hospital. What people don't understand is that the siren is about getting staff up there, not just notifying the public. There's a lot to be said for the old tech. We always talked about Frank Mitchell and how he escaped. We would *only* use sirens for escapes or if we lost control of the hospital.'

The unwelcome and sensationalist media attention took Broadmoor escapes all the way to the parliamentary agenda in the 1960s. The infamous politician Enoch Powell, then Minister of Health and MP for Wolverhampton South West, engaged in a particularly lively exchange with William van Straubenzee, MP for Wokingham, and therefore very anxious about his constituents. Van Straubenzee asked Powell whether he would make a statement on the escape of John Slater and Brian Smith from what was then Broadmoor Institution on 25th October 1961.

Enoch Powell responded that after they escaped on the evening of 25th October, they were captured again the very next morning. There was an immediate inquiry, and instructions were given for additional security measures, including certain structural alterations and increased search of patients after seeing visitors.

Van Straubenzee wasn't dropping this without a fight, however. He wanted to know whether the implement one of the patients used to escape had ever been found. He couldn't believe that the searching of patients after they had received visitors wasn't just a basic practice that had been standard for ages. It does seem fairly unbelievable!

Powell had to grumpily concede that the implement hadn't been found, although there was no proof it was a visitor who brought it in. He said up to that point it was the practice to search those under maximum security arrangements at Broadmoor after seeing visitors, but that was going to be extended to other patients after Slater and Smith's bold escape.

Van Straubenzee cropped up again in an urgent parliamentary debate he called, requesting that the Parliamentary Secretary to the Ministry of Health join it. What he wanted to talk about, and raise detailed questions about, was the escape of Richard Upcher from Broadmoor that had taken place on 21st February, with the siren going off at about 11:05pm.

During previous escapes Broadmoor had come under heavy fire for the warning siren not being sounded anywhere near quickly enough, and that was causing people who lived near Broadmoor a lot of fear and anxiety.

He made reference to some interesting gossip about Broadmoor night staff affecting their working abilities by moonlighting in day jobs at factories and other places of employment. Van Straubenzee was right to raise concerns about the night staff being overstretched. He was also worried that the fact that Richard Upcher was in Broadmoor because of being arraigned for armed robbery was both very important and a fact that had not been spread about enough. He also criticised the fact that it took far too long after the seemingly rather quiet and subdued Upcher had escaped for word to be put out that he was, in fact, highly dangerous and criminally insane.

This vital information would empower his constituents, because that knowledge would let them take precautions really quickly in the event of an escape. All too aware of the nature of the patients he was dealing with, he pointed out that protecting their children was of supreme importance, but also, locking up garages where fugitives could hide, taking the keys out of their cars and hiding bicycles in the house which could otherwise be nabbed by a passing Broadmoor escapee.

Following the previous escape, he described suggestions being made by a community living in fear, who had requested an 'all-clear' signal from the warning sirens to go off too. He said that everyone, but especially older people living alone in the surrounding towns and countryside, was in a state of abject terror while an escapee was still known to be at large.

For all of them, it would be amazing to have a siren that could notify them when these escapees had been safely rounded up and taken back to Broadmoor again.

While no system of security at Broadmoor or anywhere else could offer a total guarantee of no failures or escapes, the warning system was under heavy scrutiny for years for being ineffective. Despite huge efforts going into it technically, it often could not be heard even in the surrounding Berkshire countryside, let alone Southampton, somewhere that was stated as an aspiration by the tech team. This led to the decision being taken that sirens linked with the central one should be established in the population centres of Wokingham and Bracknell.

The warning link sirens seemed to have disappeared into a massive black hole of bureaucracy, thanks to a deadening combination of the Ministry and the local authority. Those two stumbling blocks to progress certainly persisted far beyond the 1960s as well.

The year 1981 was a bad one for killer escapes from Broadmoor, and was one of the things that marked the start of a wild decade in the hospital's history. Alan Reeve, aged 32, managed to escape from Broadmoor by using a grappling hook attached to a makeshift rope, which was enough to allow him to get over an 18-foot inner wall. Some convenient scaffolding on the outer wall allowed him to scale it with relative ease. Reeve's escape came less than three weeks after another patient, a child killer, managed to escape using a rope he had made out of knotted bedsheets.

Reeve was no angel either. He had been sent to Broadmoor at the tender age of 15 for clubbing and stabbing one of his friends to death. Four years later, he had managed to strangle a patient within the hospital. When he escaped he was carrying 11 stone on his six-foot frame. Not the best person to be running around Crowthorne.

The police set up road blocks in Surrey and Hampshire as well as the Berkshire epicentre. Prior to his hospital break-out, Reeve had written to the then Home Secretary, William Whitelaw, complaining that the Home Secretary had blocked his release even though he'd had a good psychologist's report. In this sense the police suspected he might have been trying to prove a point. Maybe he was just despairing of even getting out of Broadmoor unless he tried to do something about it himself. The police also reckoned he had probably had someone on the outside helping him to escape.

Reeve certainly had a dramatic way of proving a point, and the idea of him having outside assistance is intriguing and now difficult to get to the bottom of. Who wanted him out? The most plausible theory seems to be a girlfriend, and in the past Reeve had certainly embraced a private life in his spells between incarceration.

After the press sensation of his arrest, trial and conviction, Kenneth Erskine somehow pretty much stayed out of the headlines during his long Broad-moor stay, with a couple of notable exceptions. The first of these was in 1994, when Erskine became one of the historically rather sizeable number of patients who have managed to escape from Broadmoor.

While in Heatherwood Hospital in Ascot, Berk-shire, for an X-ray on a suspected broken finger, Erskine asked if he could go to the toilet. Some bungling followed. While a female nurse checked a cubicle, Erskine legged it, and the male nurse escorting him got separated from him in the packed casualty ward. Erskine's escape lasted less than an hour. He was recaptured by police in Ascot High Street, having run across the racecourse trying to evade them. He didn't put up a fight though, and back he went to Broadmoor.

Embarrassingly, another Broadmoor killer, Anthony Pilditch, had escaped *the day before*. He also made use of a toilet trip, the sort of ploy a toddler might use, to evade his escorts during a rather dubious-sounding 'rehabilitation shopping' trip to Reading. Pilditch nicked a load of cash, jewellery and watches, and only got caught again when he happened to need hospital admittance a week later for a dodgy heart.

Reports on these cringe-making and obviously potentially lethal escapes seemed to show very little evidence of appropriate observation and escorting methods, and no mention of handcuffs. Pilditch had ended up in Broadmoor after raping and murdering a 17-year-old waitress. To say it was inappropriate for him to have been allowed to nip to the George Hotel, Reading, toilet unaccompanied is an understatement.

When Gwen Adshead first went to Broadmoor as a young trainee psychiatrist, some men were still quite interested in escaping, but according to her in 2018, no men were interested in escaping. She explained:

'The security team now spend a lot of time chasing ghosts. They have to operate at that sort of level as if they might escape, and it has a Category B security protocol, but a lot of the guys in Broadmoor now say they need to be in a place like that, and are OK about it. And that actually creates a problem in terms of providing rehabilitation.'

It is clear that over the years, though protecting the people who call the towns and villages around Broadmoor home is a huge priority, it has not always been possible or successful.

Dr Pat McGrath, the legendary final medical super-intendent of Broadmoor, had a saying that has always stuck in Clive Bonnet's head: 'You cannot nurse them if they are running across Bagshot Heath.'

The priority *has* to be security. Always.

As Clive recalls it, his formal nurse training involved lots of education and training based around storytelling. There was *always* a moral to the stories told. One famous fable he called 'checking the hot plates', referring to the incident mentioned earlier, where Upcher escaped in a hot plate drawer. That story was re-told time and time again to trainee staff. The daily routines were easily exploited by patients, and staff had to be incredibly attuned to them.

Another remarkable example Clive gave us was what he called the 'bar check'. You used the M1 – the longer key to tap the bars of the secure accommoda-tion. If the bar has been sawed, it makes a completely different noise. Clive was taught that there was always a *reason* doing things in Broadmoor the way they had always been done.

Ward-based education was of course incredi-bly significant too, and was more about practical training. It was not theoretical – the tutors were all nurses. Theory was grounded in practice. Training became easy because you were *absorbed*. Despite all this training it was still a struggle to prepare you for the full realisation that 'points of hesitation could mean somebody's life'.

Clive described a situation in the early days of his career where they had minimal staff. He had to do the rounds at night in Block 4. There were seven staff, 30 patients, and you had to go down with your torch: 'You had to hand in your key because the orders were, if anything happens, lock the door. With yourself inside. That was the process.'

Clive Bonnet stood on point duty for an escape an astonishing four times in his long service. The patient was right behind him once! During an escape they would call on the army for assistance and they issued a pickaxe handle to each man taking part in the search. In 1982, during the Alan Reeves' escape, Clive was checking cars.

Clive remains tickled by the fact that he ended up in a press photo captioned 'Village of Fear'. Another patient, James Lang, made his escape with Reeve, but Lang twisted his ankle going over the wall. 'Village of Fear' came out in *The Sun*. Decades later, Clive describes Lang and Reeves as 'quite naughty boys'.

No matter how tight you make external security, there are always patients who want to escape. There's a danger now of an immobile hostage. If it takes 20 years to make a plan, they will find a way to do it. There's lots to be said for security, but security also affects the all-important and hard-won rapport.

Chapter 11

Exploiting the vulnerable

It might be hard to think of the inmates of Broadmoor as being vulnerable. These are dangerous men, violent men, criminally insane men. But the men – and, in earlier years, women – who have been admitted to Broadmoor deserve to be treated humanely, no matter what they did on the outside. However, that is not always the case.

In 2010, Rhoda Sibanda, a nurse working on Epsom Ward, was given a suspended sentence, and had to sign the sex offenders register after having a sexual relationship with a Broadmoor patient. She gave the patient a ring and wrote him love letters. This was despite the patient being a convicted rapist and arsonist. Another staff member blew the whistle on them after he saw them sneaking towards a laundry room together.

A strange story emerged in 2012, too, when a Broadmoor staff member and trained martial artist Tracy Morton wrote a letter to a patient telling him that he was 'very special', including some sweets, and a request that he eat the letter after reading it.

She gave it to a junior colleague to pass on, who reported the incident, leading to her dismissal. She had also been prone to four-letter abuse of patients. During Morton's tribunal, another worrying story emerged. She had been mentoring a therapy assistant, not named during the tribunal, who had been accused of having sex with two patients. A note from a patient suggested that the assistant had sex with him and with another patient, and he was keen to know whether he ought to have an HIV test. This assistant, who Morton was a friend and mentor to, was only moved on when another post became available, despite the severity of these accusations, which arose in Christmas 2009, but she did not move on to another role until the summer of 2010.

However, the worst offender was the most famous, and – for a time – one of the best-known and well-loved celebrities in Britain: Jimmy Savile.

Whether it was at Stoke Mandeville, Leeds General Infirmary or Broadmoor, Jimmy Savile knew how to get to the heart of medical institutions whose purpose was to care for vulnerable people. His technique was always the same: slick, sick and well-honed. Savile charmed his way in by befriending senior health officials. The endgame was the sexual abuse of vulnerable patients, often in their hospital beds.

Savile's first contact with Broadmoor is a great example of his ability to charm his way into highly secure medical institutions. The story goes that having received a number of fan letters from the hospital's patients, in 1968 Savile telephoned Broadmoor's entertainments officer and suggested he should visit. Shortly afterwards, the head of Broadmoor at that time, Dr Pat McGrath, asked Savile to provide entertainment and organise celebrity appearances for patients in a move that he thought would generate positive publicity for the hospital.

Now, what we have discovered is that there is an ambiguity here. Was he approached and invited? Or did he make an approach and was accepted? Gwen Adshead told us wryly that 'no one will now admit to being the one that invited Jimmy Savile to the hospital'. So, it seems that history has been re-written and now the accepted 'truth' is that Savile approached the hospital himself. He groomed and manipulated people who arguably ought to have been able to identify a more sinister agenda. He obtained a set of keys. He wanted to be their entertainment officer, and eventually to help run the place.

Crucially, what is clear is that within weeks, Savile had been handed an unofficial role as 'honorary entertainments officer'. Apparently, one of his actions in this role was to organise all-female discos as a dubious form of 'therapy'. His ward access allowed him access to young female patients away from the staff for 'lasses-only' seventies dance parties. He had an apartment in Broadmoor's grounds.

Savile rapidly won the trust of Pat McGrath, the ultimate authority figure for the hospital, and had been allowed a car parking space just outside the security perimeter. He would arrive unannounced, often bringing his caravan. His presence divided Broadmoor staff, but they were united by a reluctance to challenge the authority of Dr McGrath, who viewed handing Savile the keys in such a high secure environment as the highest mark of trust the management could offer.

This trust made Savile very powerful. In 1987, his access to Broadmoor went up another level. Just as he had gained the trust of Pat McGrath in 1968, this time Savile charmed Cliff Graham, a senior civil servant who had met the DJ on his first visit to Broadmoor. As part of sweeping changes to mental health policy, Graham made Savile a leading member of a task force directly involved in running Broadmoor.

Savile boasted about his friends in high places with celebrity visits, including several by Diana, Princess of Wales. Other duped luminaries included the seventies dance troupe Pan's People and the boxer Frank Bruno, who as we noted, posed for now-infamous photographs with Broadmoor patient Peter Sutcliffe, the "Yorkshire Ripper".

While he was winning over executives and ministers, Savile was also, according to some, carrying out a reign of terror on the women's wards. Female patients described how he watched and made inappropriate comments when they showered naked in front of staff. One said she believed two patients had killed themselves due to the abuse they suffered at Savile's hands. In total, at least five individuals are thought to have been sexually attacked by Savile at Broadmoor, including two patients who were subjected to repeated assaults.

When Jonathan was working towards access from 2009 to 2014 for the subsequent ITV television documentary series one of his great champions was his boss at the time at ITV, leading British arts figure Lord Melvyn Bragg. Bragg has always held a wide range of interests and positions, including Chancellor of Leeds University, as well as being a highly successful writer, broadcaster and television executive. In 2009 he was up in Leeds, connected to his work at Leeds University, and found himself at an event along with Jimmy Savile. To make conversation, he told Savile that we were engaged in access to the hospital for a landmark television series.

Bragg explained subsequently to Jonathan that the mood turned sour as soon as he had uttered the words. Savile instantly became highly aggressive. 'I won't let you,' he said. 'They've been through enough, those people. You won't make that series, I won't let you. I won't have it.'

Whether Savile contacted ministers or attempted to derail the project, we don't know. It certainly did take a number of years and a change of minister after that meeting before we received our green light.

Savile was hiding in plain sight and acting with brazen impunity. One of those female patients, Alison Pink, alleged that he abused her at Broadmoor.

Jimmy Savile died in 2011, and it wasn't until 2012, when an ITV documentary was broadcast, that sexual abuse allegations were brought to the public's attention, leading to more people coming forward with their own stories about assault they had suffered at his hands. All this noise and all these allegations forced the governing body of Broadmoor, West London NHS Trust, to act and commission an independent report on the troubling relationship, which was published in 2014. Investigators looked into 11 allegations of sexual abuse by Jimmy Savile at Broadmoor. Kate Lampard QC, who oversaw the investigation by the Department of Health and West London Mental Health Trust, revealed that at some point during his time at Broadmoor, from 1968 to 2004, Savile was given keys which allowed him unrestricted access to ward areas, day rooms and patient rooms.

Alternative entrances to some wards allowed him to reach areas unsupervised and without the knowledge of those in charge. Some staff enforced strict security procedures and distrusted Savile's motives. Other staff were more tolerant, and failed to enforce strict security and supervision.

Dr Bill Kirkup CBE, lead investigator into allegations at Broadmoor Hospital, said, 'There were 11 allegations of sexual abuse directly related to Broadmoor by Savile. Six involved patients at the time, two were staff and three minors. Two were male and nine were female. We were able to test in detail the veracity of six of these accounts and we concluded all of them were sexually abused by Savile. Two, both patients, were subjected to repeated assaults.'

Another five accounts were reported to Operation Yewtree – the codename for the police investigation into Savile and others – but the identity of the victim was unknown and could not be traced. Dr Kirkup added that fewer people had come forward from Broadmoor Hospital than elsewhere.

He said: 'The numbers are likely to be a significant underestimate of the true picture. Patients were very strongly discouraged from reporting at the time. The surprise is so many did find the courage to come forward.

'Taking all that into account, there seems to me no doubt that Savile was an opportunistic sexual predator throughout the time he was associated with Broadmoor.'

Savile's power and influence had such a stranglehold that he was able to get his inexperienced and under-qualified friend Alan Franey appointed as Broadmoor's general manager. In addition to being a way of having another supporter inside the wall, it also sent out a clear message that Savile was deeply involved in the running of the hospital, with the power to hire and fire. He was becoming immune to any challenge.

The report into Savile's abuse at Broadmoor showed security systems and procedures were improved while Savile was associated with the hospital. His right to keys was not formally withdrawn until 2009, but the use of personal keys was taken away after new security arrangements were introduced in 1998. Savile stopped visiting the hospital after being told how these new arrangements would operate in 2004.

Jimmy Savile's last visit was in 2004, when they pulled his keys. He was denied access for many years. Now disgraced and deceased, Savile's toxic brand lingers on. There is an apocryphal story about Robert Maudsley blocking the door with a pinball machine that Jimmy Savile had gifted when Maudsley committed the murder that opens this book. Savile insisted on delivering the pinball machine to the patients. Doors are perhaps Broadmoor's most fundamental and invaluable resource. What were the doors that Jimmy Savile notoriously had the keys to? Were they the same doors used to bring in the pinball machine he insisted on delivering to the patients against the hospital's better judgement? It was pieces from this pinball machine that were used by fabled former patient Robert Maudsley. It's all part of the sordid Savile narrative, which has left a profound and lasting stain on the British cultural landscape.

There was a time when Broadmoor used to have dances, fetes and charity football tournaments. Given these past security breaches and the brazen impunity with which Savile was permitted to operate, Broadmoor's current profound concern about permeability and indiscretion is perhaps understandable. Protecting patient and staff confidentiality is always very high on Broadmoor's agenda. Evidence of wrongdoing being exposed at an employment tribunal or in court is something that the hospital can work hard to learn lessons from and take preventative measures against. A more difficult thing to control is staff indiscretion, press leaks, and negative stories emerging in a misleading way. It creates hugely difficult issues for a hospital staff who are overwhelmingly committed, competent and discreet.

Steve Shrubb, Chief Executive for West London Mental Health NHS Trust –WLMHT – and the executive in charge when we made the ITV series, said the following as part of an apology to Savile's victims: 'For 150 years Broadmoor has provided treatment to some of the most mentally ill patients in England. Broadmoor Hospital is often the first safe place our patients have found in their lives. Lives which have often been filled with violence, neglect and abuse. This is what makes the reading of the detailed investigations into the abuse so disturbing.'

He added that although it had been 15 years since the abuse Savile put his victims through it was only now the full extent of his behaviour has been uncovered. Shrubb said: 'For all those years patients and staff who were abused by Savile have kept silent. Some from fear that they would not be believed. Who would believe a dangerous mentally ill patient against a national hero? Or because of fear that they would be punished for speaking out. I want to say thank you to those who were abused by Jimmy Savile in Broadmoor, you have shown great strength and bravery in speaking out about these awful events. I realise my comments can't heal the injuries that Jimmy Savile has inflicted on you through his callous abuse of your vulnerability but I can offer my most sincere and heartfelt apologies on behalf of Broadmoor Hospital and the WLMHT.'

Deputy Director of Nursing Jimmy Noak attended Jimmy Savile's funeral. He did so because at this point there was no suggestion of the abuse allegations that were to come. It was only after Savile's death and burial that the allegations came to light, although there had been mounting concerns about his level of access to the hospital, and successful efforts made to restrict it, long before the allegations emerged.

Through our many years of research we detected quite a mixed view of Jimmy Savile amongst staff. Not all of them subscribe to the notion that he was all bad by any means. Ultimately, as Gwen Adshead emphasises, Jimmy Savile was a massive star, and Broadmoor was more than happy to collaborate with him for many years.

Dr Adshead takes a characteristically alternative, contrarian view on Savile.

'He was a complicated man,' she told us. 'He was someone who wanted to be seen to be a good guy. Seen to be doing great and good things that no one else can do. The TV show *Jim'll Fix It* was a metaphor for "I can do anything". I can do what no one else can do – make dreams come true. He clearly was a man who was very preoccupied with his self-image and very grandiose. Very smart. He was invited to Broadmoor at the time, it was all part of the rehabilitation of the hospital as something more medical. Getting away from it being a prison or an asylum. Nobody wants to now admit to being the person that asked him but he was invited to come and visit and make the hospital seem more outward-seeming and he did.

'He probably did have keys because he was a bigwig and why wouldn't you give him keys? But I have to tell you that I don't believe that he abused any of the women in Broadmoor. Quite frankly, I don't think any of them would have attracted him in any way. I think he liked conquests but I don't think he would have wanted any of our women and I think it is very unlikely. Now we know what we know, I would be much more worried about corrupt relationships with the nurses and corrupting and inappropriate discussions with the likes of Mr Kray and with Mr Sutcliffe.

'He kept himself apart, didn't he?, and in many ways, he had a very sad life. And I think fundamentally, he was someone who could only gain pleasure by exploiting or degrading other people. It is clear from the records that he was interested in vulnerable young women and the idea that you have to do what I say because I am Jimmy Savile! When you are in my position, you can have any pussy you want – rather Trump-like in a way. It was all much more to do with power than abhorrent sexual desires. He might have been interested in seeing how far he could push things.'

She argued that many of the stories of Jimmy Savile are 'histrionic'.

'What happens is that you get a very distorted story. I heard a talk given by one of the police officers who was leading the investigation and he described when Savile had been visiting a hospital and all the nurses were lined up and he had grabbed one of the nurses' breasts and given them a tweak. This was the 1970s and everybody just laughed, "Oh Jimmy, he's a lad." Nobody thought that was a sexual assault at the time, the nurse would have felt embarrassed and humiliated and that was the point. As if to say, "Look what I can do and you can do fuck all about it and you all have to laugh".'

She acknowledges that Savile's goal was the humiliation and shaming of women, and his demonstration that it was within his power to make them feel that way. She also acknowledges that he was operating in a very different environment, with a mindset that is now very difficult to imagine ourselves back into.

There were very few people like Jimmy Savile in Broadmoor as they are too damaged, she explained. 'Mental illness doesn't do that to you. People like Jimmy Savile go to prison now as people don't think of being like that as mental illness. So the people we have in Broadmoor now are grossly disabled by their mental illness and who after a while get into the role of a patient and can't get out of it. They manage to restrain themselves from hitting people for a while and then they go to a medium secure unit and then they have a stand-up row with a member of nursing staff or maybe they hit somebody and then they get sent back.'

Many politicians have come to regret their acceptance of Savile's forays and free access into Broadmoor over the years, once the inquiry into his sexual abuse of NHS patients was underway. Former Health Minister Edwina Currie expressed support for Savile's promises to confront the Prison Officers' Association about working practices. She issued an effusive press release which ended: 'He is an amazing man and has my full confidence.'

Savile boasted that he was 'running the hospital' at Broadmoor partly on the basis of his presence on a taskforce that had been sanctioned by Currie and senior civil servants. This conspiracy of silence, or at the very least, apathy, went all the way to the very top. Even former Prime Minister Margaret Thatcher's friendship with Savile spanned many years.

The 1980s was an extraordinary era in so many ways for the whole of Britain, and Broadmoor is no exception. It is a mark of how far Broadmoor has changed that all the descriptions of the time seem so bizarre and extreme and utterly extraordinary now.

Chapter 12

Day-to-day life in Broadmoor

Many staff and patients talk of Broadmoor as a village. Calling it a village gives Broadmoor a sense of community for both patients and staff, makes it less threatening, less judgemental, a better place in which to administer and undergo treatment.

Because for all its notoriety, Broadmoor is a working hospital, and much of its day-to-day life, especially on the assertive rehab wards, follows a set routine. After all, the patients need to be fed, they need to undergo treatment, they need to exercise and find things to do to fill in their time. There is a saying 'There is time and then there is Broadmoor time'. For the less unwell, who are acutely aware of their surroundings, it is often agonisingly slow.

To combat this, Broadmoor offers a range of extracurricular activities in its well-equipped carpentry, and arts and crafts workshops, music studios and extensive kitchen garden. They have a very different feel to other parts of the hospital: calm, sociable, industrious. The art and woodwork areas are housed in a low-built, single-storey, large building with easy listening music playing in the background, and the atmosphere is surprisingly calm and relaxing. Former inmate Dante, before he died, was a devoted and regular user of the arts and crafts areas of the hospital.

There is almost an aura of the optimistic and well-organised feeling of the design and technology department in a secondary school. It even smells the same, all glue, and cut wood and the hot smell of metal having been freshly cut. The patients clearly find enormous satisfaction in their craft. There are paintings hanging on the walls, racks and racks of finished artworks, wood carvings, metalwork, hung and displayed with pride, but there are no proud parents coming on parents' evening to see little Johnny's work, it's not that kind of place. Still, that is how it is modelled. And, in fact, some of the patients looked to be barely out of school.

There are lethal-looking implements everywhere, which feels totally at odds with the airport-style entrance to the hospital, where every item is confiscated so that it can't be lost or stolen and repurposed into a weapon. For patients, access to this area of the hospital is a hard-won privilege. The patients that are present seem highly aware of what a pleasant and normal environment they are in. Only the most stable and calm are allowed in.

One young patient, probably in his early twenties, told us, 'I like it here, I've made some good work. They sell some of it. I'm always in here – ask him!' The last remark was directed to a nearby staff member, who acknowledged the patient and obviously was accustomed to joining him in a bit of banter. It was a clear example of the therapeutic and normalising power of the workshop in action.

Patients who are well enough to go to work can make goods that are on sale to the public. The hospital's front desk houses a collection of birthday cards, and Christmas and Valentine's Day cards, depending on the time of year. The money they make from sales goes towards buying the materials and equipment used to produce the goods in the first place. It may seem strange to buy artwork produced by a patient in Broadmoor, but those who purchase the goods are not just those with a macabre interest in criminals, but families of those inside, their friends, and locals.

There are so many obvious benefits to this programme, also known as 'Broadcrafts'. Patients can sell their work if it is good enough, which raises their self-esteem by literally showing them their 'market value'. It can involve teamwork. Importantly, as staff like Clive Bonnet would agree, it gets them off the ward. There's a rhythm to their day and reason for their existence. One memorable craft project involved patients designing 20 lovely Scandinavian pine birdboxes, which ended up having starlings nest in them.

The creation of a working environment for patients gives a sense of structure to the day, as well as allowing them to socialise in a controlled context. Many patients have never experienced this kind of structure and routine before, or the sense of a 'normal' working life. For many, it's a major step on the road to recovery, as well as a vital self-esteem boost. The sense of productive manual labour and a tangible end product is for some patients a novel sensation. With gruelling and emotionally draining treatments, leading to the shock of understanding the crime that landed them in Broadmoor, patients need downtime. Healing. Distraction.

In 2012, Broadmoor held a week-long exhibition of work in the Hospital's Central Walk. The exhibition offered workshops and displays from each of the ten areas of Broadmoor's Vocational Services Programme, which are made up of carpentry, print, radio, horticulture, engineering, enterprises, construction, pottery and silver clay.

There are plenty of themed art competitions, including one centred on the big move and one for the best decorated ward at Christmas. Patients can write for the patient magazine. A long-running publication, one of its most moving features is poems by patients, often highly eloquent and emotional.

The winning poem, 'Love is a Funny Thing', in the Winter 2010 edition of the magazine was particularly striking and skilful. It urged the reader to love the life they are living, while the runner-up's poem 'Time' described its subject matter as something that goes by slowly, minute by minute, for many, but for the author, 'it just stands still'.

We saw with our own eyes the patients' role in governance in patient forums and so on. Various sports are on offer and a football tournament was planned to celebrate the move to the new building, whenever it eventually happens.

The constant to-ing and fro-ing on the assertive rehab wards can make you forget that this is Broadmoor. Soon enough, however, reminders crop up of exactly where you have found yourself.

In the kitchens, for instance, each item has to be carefully accounted for, as what is a common domestic object in the outside world can become a lethal weapon in the possession of many Broadmoor patients.

Just like a village, Broadmoor has its own shop, a food shop, which is at least in part run by patients. Patients can go to the shop once a week, if they show good behaviour. It is a windowless and bleak environment, seemingly modelled on a Londis or Spar. Pop music blares out from a radio. On our visits, we found it to be pretty understocked and mostly junk food: sweets, crisps and chocolates. Packets of biscuits lie on plastic racks. Obese patients waddle through, spending small sums of money on fattening junk. There is not much for them to spend their cash on except food from the shop. Some patients might eat a couple or even three ready meals on top of what they eat in the canteen. It's a triple whammy of medication, ready cash and boredom.

It offers a striking insight into a more domestic side of their hospitalisation. Patients walk round with little baskets brimming with confectionery. In the absence of tobacco, alcohol or intimate relationships, food is their only pleasure.

One of the side effects of medication is increased appetite and many of the patients are severely overweight. Managing obesity at Broadmoor is really hard. Many patients are on antipsychotics such as clozapine and olanzapine. More than three quarters of patients put on olanzapine develop significant weight gain in the first 12 months. Indeed, the weight gain that antipsychotics can cause can be so severe that it is a major factor in why patients refuse medication.

Antipsychotics stimulate appetite so that the inmates feel more hungry, and end up consuming more calories than they burn. However, a side effect of antipsychotics can be low mood and lack of energy (often symptoms that patients are already showing anyway), which can make it difficult to be active and burn the excess calories that they consume on the antidepressants.

Unsurprisingly, the rate of obesity and diabetes in Broadmoor is high. In Broadmoor, about 20 to 25 per cent of patients have diabetes, compared with just 6 per cent in the general population. As we've seen, some medications for mental health issues have a side effect of weight gain. There is also a close relationship between the gene that causes diabetes and the gene that causes schizophrenia. People with long-term schizophrenia are three times more likely to have diabetes. This association was attributed to the generally poor diet and fitness of the group as well as the use of antipsychotic medication. A landmark study by King's College London in 2017 indicated that shared genetic risk also had an important role.

This means that catering in Broadmoor is even more complex than in other hospitals. Patients are still expected to enjoy a varied menu, with all their dietary requirements taken into account, and all this on a tight budget. The caterers also need to factor in that some patients may be too unwell to eat, and some patients may eat too much.

For the 200 or so male patients, the catering staff include four chefs, four porters and a supervisor. The team make an effort to provide good, nutritional food for the patients, and to keep fat levels down. The catering resembles school dinners as much as anything: sandwiches and baguettes, pasta, pies, omelettes, rice, salads, jacket potatoes and quite a lot of fish and seafood. There are veggie options of course, not just for health reasons but as an easy route through the dietary requirements of different faiths. Yoghurt and fruit feature on the pudding menu but sometimes a tastier, more calorific option creeps in.

Meals are served early, rather like an old people's home. There is a cold breakfast. Lunch appears on the wards at 12.15pm. Dinner is served at 5pm, with the option of a tepid drink or a snack later.

When it comes to the food, the hospital is at pains to indicate that there is a healthy living agenda, and they are trying to address obesity by restricting the availability of junk food, which is undermined somewhat by the availability of junk food in the shop. Given that the medication for the usual range of Broadmoor mental illnesses ratchets up appetite and cravings, they may be fighting a losing battle ...

The less unwell patients have the option to order computer games, movies and music to keep them occupied in their rooms. In 2010, reports emerged that five patients had spent thousands of pounds in benefits on pricey sound equipment to learn how to be DJs. The patients in question were Anthony Joseph, William Jaggs, Jamie Limbrick and Barrington McKenzie, all convicted murderers in their mid-twenties. The fifth was Alex Candiotis, who had tried to saw open a nurse's throat while in Broadmoor, having committed a string of violent offences to justify admission in the first place. There are arguments for patients having access to expensive tech – it staves off boredom, it provides distraction for them, it offers training for a job outside of the prison – and arguments against. The equipment is expensive, after all, and it can seem galling to some that these people are leading what might appear on the outside to be a cushy life when their victims haven't been so lucky.

The more idealistic aspects of the pastoral care at Broadmoor have of course attracted controversy over the years. Matt Slater's mischievous 2005 piece for the *News of the World* attempted to push pretty much every button of public indignation: 'The Yorkshire Ripper has turned into the Incredible Hulk, thanks to slap-up meals and a cushy life inside Broadmoor.

'The last picture taken of serial psycho Peter Sutcliffe 10 years ago showed a muscular figure with neatly trimmed jet black hair and distinctive goatee beard. But today, in a sensational series of exclusive pictures, the *News of the World* reveals how he then sat back and pigged out – ballooning into a balding 17-stone slob… It is all part of an attempt to disguise himself in a chilling bid for freedom. Sutcliffe patted his huge belly and bragged: "This is because I eat so well in here and spend a lot of time just watching TV and painting.

"'It's not a bad life at all and I'm really into my cooking these days. Last week I cooked a juicy steak as big as a dinner plate with chips and mushrooms – it was delicious.

"'Now I want to make lobster thermidor – they won't have a problem with that." The hospital authorities might not mind but the British public will be outraged.'

This, of course, is a rather skewed picture of the nature of pastoral care at Broadmoor. What the public at large expects can be at odds with what the staff at Broadmoor provide. It can seem as if the patients lead a 'cushy' life, but on the other hand, rehabilitation with the result of making patients better equipped for society is a lengthy and expensive process, but it can reap rewards.

For obvious reasons they need to be highly supervised, but the Broadmoor kitchens have offered many a patient the chance to flex their inner Rick Stein, and to get off the ward. Broadmoor places great emphasis on the healing powers of food and cooking. For many, many years, the hospital has encouraged patients to learn how to cook as a great means of enhancing independence. It lets them feel pride and confidence in what they have cooked by sharing it with fellow patients on the ward.

The terrible childhoods and adolescences of many patients involved cruelty and neglect, but also a lack of real education. For many men, the Broadmoor education centre is the first place they have ever had a chance to really get their basic reading, writing and arithmetic up to scratch. This allows them to enjoy the book and DVD library. The less chronically unwell patients can have computer games, movies and music in their rooms. Patients can even study for an Open University degree. This is less with a view to using it after their release, and more to build self-esteem and stimulate them intellectually with a subject that engages them.

However, many spaces, shared or otherwise, have also been abandoned over the years. Broadmoor once housed its own thriving blacksmith's and metal workshop. This quirky facility was ultimately closed due to lack of patient interest. During some of Jonathan's first visits in 2009 he was told that patients no longer wanted to engage in traditional crafts like metalwork and apparently they just wanted to go into the computer room. Fair enough!

In the early years of the last century, the view from Broadmoor's terraces would have revealed lawns, elegant avenues of trees, flower beds and fruit trees. The patients tended these gardens, often very meticulously, over many years. The views further away were of ridiculously idyllic English fields and forests. The kitchen garden began as a Victorian ideal of self-sufficiency, with a Utopian vision of Broadmoor growing all its own food. It once covered an area of 19 acres, with, of course, a high brick wall around it. Eventually, it became overgrown and neglected.

Patients are still allowed to have a session in the garden up to ten times a week, up to 27 patients at a time. Around 14 staff help them to tend the soil, plant flowers and vegetables. This work is taken seriously and patients who show gardening prowess can even work towards a formal qualification in horticulture.

One notable communal event that Jonathan attended during the making of the TV series was a diversity workshop in a sports hall. One patient stood out. We agreed to change his name to 'Declan' to preserve his anonymity. A cross-dresser with a dark sense of humour, he joked, 'I had been in children's homes, been in secure units, been in prison and the only place I hadn't been was Broadmoor. So I thought I would come along.'

Declan was 26 when we spoke to him. He recalled being taken by his mum to an office when he was nine years old. She sat on a chair, looked him in the eye and said, 'You're not coming with me.' Then she just left. 'You're not coming with me,' that was it. The social worker said, 'You're coming with me.'

Declan was taken to a children's home. As he described it, he kept running away as he was sexually abused in the children's home by the staff and no one would listen to him.

'I ran away to London and was living on the streets and out of bins. I was charged with torture. That was my offence. Me and my co-defendant stabbed him up.

'For some reason I always wanted to be a woman but in this place you can't do that. They won't allow it. I want to be a drag queen. She's called Crystal. She is blonde and fabulous.'

Each of these wards has frequent, scheduled community meetings, which allow the patients and ward staff to talk through, work out, address and, as is often necessary, diffuse the issues arising from existence on the ward. This is necessary in terms of patients being empowered to feel that their issues are being listened to, reacted to and ideally put to bed, though of course this cannot always be the case. Catering always seemed to be top of the agenda for patients, with medication and heating coming a close second.

We were invited to the staff forum in March 2018. Individuals at the noon forum on Wednesday 7th March included Kevin Murray, Pat McKee and Ken Wakatama. There were also patient representatives.

One of them, a bloated, persistent and quite bureaucratic character in his forties, we had met before. He was more articulate than many of our peers, and was not backward in coming forward with grievances.

We had watched him lay into staff on two occasions, suggesting that they had ignored letters he had written them on what he viewed as urgent issues. Note- and letter-sending is a favourite hobby of many Broadmoor patients.

The mouthy patient at the staff forum wanted to let us know that he was concerned about his medication regime and its effect on his physical and mental well-being. As we have seen time and again, medication heals patients up to a point, but once they hit that point, they are well enough to start questioning their treatment. It can be a catch-22.

There is also a more formal monthly forum, in which hospital staff and senior managers sit with selected individuals from every ward. These meetings are less on domestic minutiae and grounded more in macro issues pertaining to the general running of the hospital. While we witnessed topics like Christmas themes and outdoor activities being covered, change and policy tweaks are also regularly on the agenda. Unsurprisingly, the new hospital has been taking up a lot of airtime and interest at the forums over the last few years.

One patient forum that we attended within assertive rehab was particularly intriguing, in some ways diverging from the norm, as well as covering many of the standard issues that are expected at these meetings.

At the forum in question, which we sat in on, Jo Dow was introduced as a new consultant on Canterbury Ward.

It soon became clear that one of the patients from Canterbury ward, 'Terry', had a massive issue with the hot – or not so hot – water. Terry made executive director Leeanne McGee a coffee, which she acknowledged was a little bit cold.

Terry claimed that it was 'almost abuse because up here are not taking patients' concerns into account … Because it is not possible to make hot soup and hot drinks.' He was extremely grumpy and aggrieved and it was quite difficult to mollify him. We later learned that he had arrived at Broadmoor after committing two brutal murders. This made the memory of sitting with him as he ranted about the temperature of warm beverages feel completely surreal.

There followed a lively and revealing discussion about patient food activities. Christmas dinner 2017 in Broadmoor was steak and chips. Fewer and fewer people are eating in the dining room, it was observed by another patient, Seth. It used to be a more communal activity, he noted with regret.

Emma had already had a proper introduction and chat to this patient we will call Seth. We suspect that the name he had adopted within Broadmoor was also a pseudonym. Having arrived in 2015, he was shy but friendly. He seemed very young but was probably mid – perhaps even late – twenties. He showed us inside his room, which he had covered in posters. Judging by the artwork, he was an Avril Lavigne and heavy metal enthusiast. Meeting him and seeing where he lived was more like visiting a student in their dorm than meeting a patient in a high secure hospital. Seth noted that they were spending more time as individuals and less time together, and that he preferred the way that things were before.

One interesting construction that Jonathan saw on an early visit to the hospital in 2009 was a gigantic and intricately built train set. The size of a small living room, it must have cost tens of thousands of pounds. It was breathtaking in its construction and attention to detail.

Jonathan stopped and looked at it for at least 15 minutes as the trains rattled around their little tracks. Points, bridges, little figures standing with flags, hills, stations and open countryside. He got lost looking at it and it was so cleverly and so beautifully put together that he has been thinking about it ever since.

In 2018, on a tour around the same area, Jonathan asked about it. Blank faces all round. Eventually, one member of staff remembered. But they could not remember who did it or where it was, just that it got taken down some years before.

There's a poignancy to this. There are the notorious patients – the Sutcliffes, the Krays, the Bronsons – who are well known to the outside world. But there are the lesser-known patients, the ones who, yes, have committed terrible acts, but who also, like the railway set, are clinically and emotionally supported daily by the staff, with care, until finally, they are deemed safe enough to be released into society, or to be returned to the general prison population. These men have been worked upon, and there has been a lot of money spent upon their treatment, and ultimately, if the treatment works, they are forgotten. But this might not be the worst thing that could happen to them. Perhaps, with all the help and care they receive, leading a quiet life, an uneventful life, a life that is no longer marked by violence or fear, is the best result they can hope for.

Chapter 13

Treatment

Broadmoor changes people. It changed us. God knows, we were pretty twitchy when we were writing about the Hatton Garden gang. A few of their associates had us nervous enough to invest in a metal baseball bat under the bed.

Meeting Broadmoor patients was another level though. We've shown the positive impact it has on many patients, even the most unwell. We've shown the staff commitment, the passion and the professionalism. However, there are also the suicides, escapes, deaths from restraint, failed rehabilitation, institutionalised staff, inappropriate relationships between staff and patients, and some pretty dire Care Quality Commission (CQC) inspection reports.

While the UK has an undeniably murky history of treating mental health, in the last few decades there seem to have been notable steps forwards. Or so we might hope. However, while public attitude and perception of mental illness might have improved, aspects of the system have not. The Centre for Mental Health estimates that 21,000 mentally ill people are currently imprisoned, making up a quarter of the prison population. That can't be good, can it?

With the shutting down of the old asylum system and cuts across the board to mental health services, many British psychiatric patients are ending up in prisons instead. Since 1986, the number of beds available for mental health patients in the UK has dropped by a staggering 75 per cent.

We ended up asking ourselves, *is Broadmoor good for your health*?

Broadmoor has certainly not always been good for our own health, in particular our blood pressure. Access over the years has been nothing short of a Kafkaesque experience. Getting ministerial sign-off took years for the TV series and then there was yet another board, another meeting, another delay. It could sometimes feel like we were patients trying to leave the hospital.

We get it. It is in the nature of the people who run the place to 'manage' everyone. Manage expectations. Control the process. They are so institutionalised that they cannot help it and they did it to us as much as they did it when we made the series, and they do it to the patients. We had a similar experience around access for this book.

Maybe we were getting institutionalised ourselves, but we certainly started to have a stronger feeling for the patients' frustrations. As far as they were concerned, in many cases, exactly what hoops did they have to jump through to get out?

Unlike a prison sentence, the patients at Broadmoor have no release date. On a psychological level, this can make them feel incredibly frustrated. Moving on from Broadmoor is a slow process. Birthdays and Christmases come and go, with no set dates for release.

What is happening in the meantime to drive them through the process?

Therapy is one way.

Group therapy usually uses groups with some kind of shared experience, often a disturbing one, and positions the discussion around that. So, for example, a violent offenders' group, with the aim of talking about those experiences, allows patients to realise that they're not the only one who feels the way they do.

Many of the patients in Broadmoor have a history of substance abuse, abuse strongly linked to their mental illness. Therapy aims to give them the skills to resist temptation. It can only do so much. A Substance Abuse Group Therapy session that was followed during the filming process had half a dozen patients sat around in a circle with a therapist standing and talking.

In attendance was 31-year-old Michael, who was suffering from paranoid schizophrenia.

'When I started hearing the voices it was amazing, I couldn't believe it. I had to run out of the house because I was scared, you understand. I was smoking cannabis heavily. It was like a living part of my head, like a demonic being speaking to me. The voice just called me a fool just now. It is like having a conscious being in your head and you just learn to live with it.'

While medication can diminish harmful voices like this, it often doesn't eradicate them.

Muktar had been in Broadmoor for two years when we spoke to him for the documentary.

'I have never seen my mum. She is in America. I have tried to find her but I don't even know her full name.'

Muktar ran away from foster care when he was 16. He was in street gangs and was selling drugs. He didn't realise he was also becoming mentally ill.

'I have had a lot of stress,' he told us. 'I kept on hearing voices and I kept on attacking people and I kept on being erratic.'

A rival gang warned him off their territory. Muktar said his dealer gave him a gun and told him to deal with them.

'When you have the weapon for the first time you think "whoa". In some ways it felt like "I am dangerous now". But on the other hand, it felt like "I am vulnerable now as well".'

Armed with a gun, Muktar returned to the estate.

'My intentions were that if I fired the gun in the air, these people would run off. But they didn't run off. They chased me to a block of flats with knuckle dusters. Cornered me. One of them got the gun and pulled it, like to try and take it off my hand. I was scared. I was thinking I was going to get killed here. So I grabbed the gun and I just remember BAM! And my finger pulling the trigger. It was the worst experience I have ever had. I had just turned 18.'

Found guilty of manslaughter, Muktar was sent to Broadmoor under a hospital order.

'I didn't know anything about this place. I was told about medication I had to take. I said, "I don't need any medication." After my first dose my voice started to reduce in intensity. Something is happening now. It was different.'

Muktar was really focused on his recovery and expressed a hope to go to university one day. He writes poetry. One particularly poignant example dealt with his dream of life on the outside, recalling his incarceration as a mistake, and expressing a deep longing to be with his family again.

Another patient we met while filming, Adam, had been out, escorted by nurses from the hospital to the medium secure unit he was hoping to move to in a couple of weeks. But there was a hold up.

As Adam explained, 'The person whose bed I am waiting for hasn't had their MOJ permission so everything has changed and gone tits up, so there isn't going to be any movement for at least two to three months.'

Adam thought that he was leaving in a week but it all changed. It was a crushing disappointment and we witnessed the impact first-hand. And, of course, it must have seemed so unfair – after all, he had done his best to get himself into a position where he could leave Broadmoor, but something that he had no control over was preventing his release.

'I ended up screaming, shouting, throwing things at my door as if to say get out because I was just about to do something. Usually when I throw things I pick the bits up and want to do something with them, but this time I didn't and it shows how far I've come. I got a lot of praise for not self-harming.'

If Adam did self-harm, it would jeopardise his chances of moving out of Broadmoor. He was caught in a vicious circle where he would do everything he could to change his circumstances, but then circumstances out of his control would hold him back, making him frustrated, lashing out, potentially harming himself, and running the risk of going right back to the start again.

Many patients have been caught up in a similar vicious circle. During a visit to Chepstow Ward, we spoke to Dr Fin Larkin, who wanted to discuss an incident involving Lenny, the inmate we discussed in Chapter 9, and another patient. Lenny had been talking about how happy he was that paedophiles are being arrested in society.

Lenny explained that he was guilty of the offence that brought him to Broadmoor: brandishing a machete towards a consultant psychiatrist and threatening to kill him. He was keen to stress, however, that he wasn't guilty of sexual crimes.

He said it felt like there was no recognition that he was a victim. And that's why he had attacked his psychiatrist.

While medication can control behaviour, such as that exhibited by Adam and Lenny, extensive therapy is also required to really *change* behaviour. It takes time. Patients undergo particular therapies depending on the nature of their offence, whether it be sex offending, violence or fire-setting.

We witnessed a group therapy session for a violent offenders' group. That session, they were discussing appropriate behaviour and boundaries. The atmosphere was calm and there were only five or six patients in the group, sitting calmly and trying their best to engage.

'What sort of actions are used within safe relationships?' the therapist asked.

A patient responded with little hesitation.

'Laughter. Talking sensible, feeling comfortable with each other.'

The other patients agreed and it felt like progress was being made.

On the other end of the spectrum, occasionally we met patients who it was very hard to envisage ever being ready for the outside world.

While researching the book, Emma was introduced to an older, bearded man sitting alone in the communal area of a ward.

A shaft of light fell across his face as he quietly, fluently, began to list a series of increasingly wild conspiracy theories. He spoke to Emma as if they had been engaged in this conversation a thousand times before. He described his belief that he was in line to the throne and that had led to a conspiracy against him, which the medical staff was conniving in.

Although not manic or clearly unwell like patients on intensive care, there was something astonishingly frightening about him, and it was difficult to know how to deal with his rant without knowing what might set him off. He was calm but highly delusional. When Emma left him, the staff member who had made the introduction simply turned to her and said, '*He's a very dangerous man.*'

That was a room that Emma was particularly glad to leave.

The combination of medication and therapy are the cornerstones of the patients' experience at Broadmoor, and they take many different forms.

Generally started near the beginning of the psychotherapy process, psychoeducation provides information and support to mental health service users. This information commonly includes advice about medication and its impact. It's about how it can alleviate their symptoms but also the side effects. It's a chance to talk through the medication plan, rather than bombarding patients, who are often incredibly confused or disturbed, with unnecessary paperwork.

This doesn't change the fact that some patients refuse medication, or would prefer not to take it, largely due to the prevalence of side effects, though there are other reasons too.

Dr Larkin told us: 'One of the difficulties about psychotic disorders is that your interpretation of reality is different. So if you genuinely believe there is nothing wrong with you and you don't need any medication, why on earth would you want to take some of the medication that would be up for discussion?'

Patients have access to a wide range of 'talking therapies'. Perhaps the most famous one is cognitive behavioural therapy – CBT – which allows patients to take a really active, practical role in addressing their illness. Then there is MBT, or mentalisation-based therapy, which helps to improve the ability of patients to comprehend both their own and other people's mental states. Our contributor to the book, Dr Gwen Adshead, was part of the team running a pilot project to see if they could improve mentalisation in violent people.

Occupational therapy is something we saw in action a lot. It's meant to create balance and structure to a patient's day through craft or manual labour. Gardening. Cookery. Art. Woodwork. On one visit we met two young patients in the workshop. One was withdrawn, introverted. He felt very uncomfortable to be in close proximity to us, and frankly, the feeling was mutual.

The other, who looked to be no more than in his mid-twenties, was keen to tell us how much he enjoyed the workshop and creating. We had read that there are fewer violent incidents in the off-ward areas, and the occupational therapy zones. Calms the savage beast, so to speak.

There is the hope that the immense physical security of Broadmoor can mean lower doses of medication are administered than in other secure units. Broadmoor's patients, like any other patients, can have side effects on some drugs and not on others. The UK has over 20 licensed antidepressants and 20 licensed antipsychotics. You would hope that there would be one to suit everyone, but of course it's trial and error.

The most common side effect of 'typical' (older-generation) antipsychotics is akathisia or, in plain English, uncontrollable muscle spasms. The most common side effect of 'atypical' (newer generation) antipsychotics is massive weight gain and extreme drowsiness.

A patient we'll call 'Anthony' said in a therapy group we sat in on: 'I've got capacity to make decisions according to the doctor. Do you think that mental health patients should be able to, while they're well, choose the treatment?'

Anthony wanted to ask his team something.

'Why do you believe I am so against antipsychotic medication? [...] It is torment. It's the debilitating effect of not being able to communicate, to be able to have internal anguish and frustrations, and no longer being able to converse with the people that you love. You lose all your friendships, you become isolated.

'Then you've got the physical side effects. You don't want to look good. Your hair goes flat and greasy. Your skin gets very poor, you put on weight, you get staring eyes. Everybody knows you're on medication.'

Anthony's comments really drove home the massive issue of whether you refuse medication and become a psychotic outcast, or take it and become a virtual zombie.

Dr Susan Young developed a now-famous 'game', the 'Secret Agent' tool. It can be played in order to judge patients' risk-taking behaviours, using information from past studies that found links between risk-taking behaviours with impulsivity and insensitivity. It also presents patients with moral decisions, and thereby helps assess patients on their empathy, altruism and moral reasoning.

It's basically a computer game where they are put in situations where they have to make decisions based on ethics and risk. Looking at their scores helps patients to understand themselves. Looking at their behaviour helps their therapists understand how to treat them. So, how does how they relate to other people in this game make them different from Joe Public?

What the medical staff at Broadmoor want their patients to achieve is 'insight', which combines using strong antipsychotic drugs and tough therapies to get patients to recognise that they have a mental illness. To see that it makes them commit criminal acts. The only way to treat a patient properly is to get right under the bonnet of the 'whats and whys' of their mental disorder.

Research into the basis of mental disorder is an important component of the work that goes on at Broadmoor. There has been some very clever work going on around brain scans to study mental illness. MRI scans can help doctors to understand why a tiny group of people amongst the mentally ill turn to extreme, frequently sadistic violence.

A study carried out by the Maudsley Hospital in South London, using neural imaging, discovered that Broadmoor patients' brains had big differences from one patient to another. Maybe that divide between personality disorder and schizophrenia is more meaningful than it seemed, because the study showed a noteworthy difference in things like fear responses. When threatened with an electric shock (that they didn't actually get), the schizophrenics were overly stimulated and those with personality disorders weren't.

Behind the scenes, in hospitals, labs and psychiatry studies across the country, work is going on to see if we can make the incurable, curable. In the meantime, how do people move on from Broadmoor?

The whole idea of prison versus Broadmoor has obsessed us in this context. Imagine if your son, brother, best mate or father commits something totally out of character, a brutal, sickening, inexplicable offence. It goes to court because they are charged with murder.

You and your solicitor have a choice. Plead diminished responsibility, or face the mercy of a judge, jury and prison sentence.

A diminished responsibility plea might seem like the easy option. 'It wasn't really me.' 'I'm not like that.' 'I'm ill.' I wasn't in my sane mind when I did it.' In fact, you may simply be swapping the certainty of a ticking clock for the uncertainty of endless medical tribunals and an indefinite hospital order. Even if you're handed down a 30-year prison sentence in court, good behaviour can mean you are out in 15 years. A hospital order means that you literally might never get out.

This highlights one of the big lies of high/medium/low security. Broadmoor say that they've managed to get the average length of time for a patient in the hospital down to five or six years on average. However, it is arguably a false statistic, because all they mean is that if you stay there for five years then get transferred to a medium security place, the slightest thing can get you sent back to Broadmoor and then the clock starts all over again. We have met patients who said it was their third or fourth time in hospital. NHS statistics make it look like the average stay is coming down whereas in fact some people are just bouncing around the system.

Jonathan made a visit alone to Ashworth, another high security hospital, and met the medical director, Ian Brady's personal doctor before Brady died. She described her most high-profile patient not by name but Jonathan knew who she was taking about. She described him as a narcissistic psychopathic sex offender, a condition for which, whether society likes it or not – and it is not what people want to hear – there is no cure. No medication. No talking cure. No treatment. After 35 years of expertise, drugs, treatment, the best possible care, if you put a child in a room with that patient, he would kill them. In one word: incurable.

So why are we spending £300,000 a year, which is the cost to put somebody in a high security hospital when there is a tacit acknowledgement that we may not be helping him, or anyone? High security hospitals regard their patients as 'vulnerable adults'. They are patients not prisoners, the staff are at pains to point out. They are being treated not punished.

Their cells are called bedrooms and their warders called nurses.

At the other end of the spectrum, when describing our book project to a relative with traditional views, he simply said, 'A bullet costs ten pence.' He could not comprehend why precious resources would be squandered on incurable psychopaths who had committed horrific crimes.

This is, of course, an extreme view. And we come back to the question we asked at the start of this chapter – *Is Broadmoor good for your health?* In Ian Brady's case, being in a high security hospital made no difference to him, as medication and talking therapies couldn't help him, it was neither good nor bad for his health. The question that arises, then, is whether he had any control over what he did? If he had no control over his behaviour, could he be held responsible for his actions?

While Broadmoor can't be said to have been good for our health, there are patients who have benefited from the medication and talking therapies they've undergone. Rehabilitation is always the aim, and it's only in the rarest cases that a patient receives no benefit at all.

Chapter 14

A very English scandal

Broadmoor is the most infamous high security hospital in the world. It's by no means the only one though, not even in the UK. Broadmoor is one of three high security hospitals in England and Wales. The other two are Rampton, in the north-east in Nottinghamshire, and Ashworth, in the north-west, in Merseyside. These three hospitals combined employ over 3,000 staff, caring for about 750 patients. There is also Carstairs, in Scotland.

Rampton Secure Hospital is the biggest of the three, caring for almost half of those patients, while also being the sole provider of high secure care for women and men with a learning disability in the country, of which it holds beds for 50 of each sex. Additionally, it holds the National High Secure Deaf Unit, which provides an additional ten beds for deaf men. Opened in 1912, Rampton was built in just three years to the design of Frances William Troup, and was originally intended as an overflow for Broadmoor. Rampton had small beginnings, with just 40 women and 88 men across three wards. All of them had transferred from Broadmoor.

Built in idyllic and deliberately remote settings, Rampton is surrounded by fields and woodland. Its nearest neighbour is an unlikely one: five minutes' drive away lies Sundown Adventure Land, a children's theme park aimed at the under-tens. Today, Rampton has more staff than Broadmoor and Ashworth combined.

Rampton grew rapidly as a space in the early decades of the 20th century. Its process of expansion involved retaining some of the pretty Victorian buildings, when they were still fit for purpose, but also adding buildings in the interwar period and then, in 2011, adding the modern, rather stylish, Mike Harris Centre and David Wilson Unit. At one point Rampton had a farm with over 500 pigs and 600 chickens. Staff at Rampton had dwelt in cottages on the campus, and rules that allowed for them to live offsite were only relaxed in 1939. The staff-to-patient ratio wasn't great, which is probably in part behind the alarming fact that in 1939 alone, they had 42 escapes.

However, in the sixties there was major investment in sports facilities, including a gymnasium, outdoor arena, and, later, a swimming pool. This was followed by dedicated patient classrooms in the 1970s, and a staff education centre in 1976. Rampton's male and female patients are allowed to socialise at some mixed events. They have access to activities similar to those available at Broadmoor, including arts, music and crafts, and a high-tech multi-sensory and relaxation room.

Rampton also, however, has its 'Peaks Unit' for those with severe personality disorders. These rooms are regarded as 'suicide safe', with mattresses made from material that is too tough to rip out, and heat resistant, while the bed frames are made from moulded fibre glass that can withstand damage and are difficult to break anything off from. The hospital has more than 900 CCTV security cameras.

Like Broadmoor, Rampton has had many patients who have received national media coverage. There is the ubiquitous Charles Bronson; Ian Ball, who tried to kidnap Princess Anne in 1974; Beverley Allitt, the notorious so-called 'Angel of Death', who was charged with four murders and 22 accounts of attempted murder against children while working as a nurse in Grantham Hospital. Allitt is believed to have suffered from Munchausen's syndrome, a rare disorder in which a person fakes illness for attention. This became Munchausen's syndrome by proxy when she began to harm, and kill, children for attention.

Rampton has cared for serial killers such as Mark Rowntree, who killed four people in Yorkshire over a week in 1976. It has seen cannibals, such as Stephen Griffiths and Peter Bryan, dismemberers, such as Thomas McDowell, who in 2002 murdered a German rabbi and cut up his corpse with a ripsaw. Some of these figures have spent time in all three of England's high security mental hospitals, seemingly bounced between them.

Rampton has also turned notable killers back to the mainstream prison system. Notably, Ian Huntley, who with Maxine Carr murdered two ten-year-old girls in Cambridgeshire in 2002. While originally placed in Rampton after his arrest, Huntley was later transferred to a mainstream prison after a report from psychologist Dr Christopher Clark found him not to be suffering from mental illness.

Even by these bleak standards, one of the more disturbing cases at Rampton is Stephen Griffiths, the self-titled 'Crossbow Cannibal'. Griffiths was born in 1969 and had a troubled childhood. His mother had sex with men in front of him and had criminal convictions. First arrested, aged just 17, after attacking a shopkeeper with a knife, he told psychiatrists and probation officers at the time he fantasised about being a serial killer. He shot birds with an air pistol and dissected them. He read and watched videos about serial killers endlessly, and developed substance abuse issues.

In 2009, he killed two prostitutes in Yorkshire. He cut their bodies apart in his bath before he cooked and ate bits of them. His third victim, Suzanne Blamires, managed to escape his flat. He chased her and shot her with a crossbow, and the CCTV footage of this horrific murder led to Griffiths' arrest. On noticing the camera, Griffiths raised a glass. Whether he was toasting the death, or acknowledging that he had been caught, is unknown. He appears to have been in Rampton ever since.

Another Rampton long-term resident 'Bruce Lee', born George Peter Dinsdale, is Britain's second most prolific serial killer after Harold Shipman. He was convicted of killing 26 people through horrendous acts of arson. Astonishingly, he was only 19. Like many of the patients discussed in this book, Lee had a horrific childhood. His mother was a prostitute who couldn't care for him, so he ended up in children's homes. He was epileptic, with mobility issues. When he was 19, he changed his surname to Lee, his stepfather's surname. His first name became Bruce after the martial artist and movie star.

Lee was only arrested after volunteering insistently to be questioned about a fire in which three young boys died, known as the Selby Street Fire. He then confessed to it, along with starting nine other local fires, killing 26 people in total. In 2005, he married another Rampton patient, Anne-Marie Davison, 31, who he met at one of the hospital's discos, where male and female patients are allowed to mix. Lee hit the press in 2016 when he was allowed out for a stroll near the facility, apparently being allowed to walk amongst unsuspecting members of the public, including children. He appears to still be at Rampton to this day, serving a life sentence.

Ashworth Hospital is the smallest of the three high security hospitals in England, with less than 200 patients, although there are beds for up to 228. It is also the youngest of the three, having opened in the 1970s. Patients at Ashworth have a shorter average stay than at Broadmoor, just five years. The figure is pushed up by a small group of more long-term patients. Managed by Mersey Care NHS Foundation Trust, Ashworth offers many of the same type of rehabilitative services as Broadmoor and Rampton. There is an art room, a staff and patient reading group, a vegetable patch, chickens, and even a cricket pitch.

Ashworth has been home to a number of high-profile patients. Dale Cregan, known as 'One-Eye' due to his left eye being carved out by a knife, murdered four people with a variety of guns and M75 grenades, including two female police officers after ambushing them with a fake 999 call. Mark Corner, who murdered two women not long after being released from Fazakerley Mental Hospital in 2003, leading to outcry over why he had been discharged early. Richard Gwilym, or 'The Cardiff Ripper', who killed five people before his capture.

The most notable patient in Ashworth's history, however, is Moors murderer Ian Brady, who with Myra Hindley tortured and killed five children before burying their bodies on Saddleworth Moor. The deaths of Pauline Reade, John Kilbride, Keith Bennett, Lesley Ann Downey and Edward Evans are one of the most disturbing crimes in British history and have left a lasting scar on the psyche of the

nation. Pat McGrath, former medical superintendent at Broadmoor, refused to allow Ian Brady to be
admitted, describing him as one of only two men he
had ever met who was not sick, but evil. Brady was
therefore admitted to Ashworth, where he remained
until his death in 2017. Throughout his time there he
made it clear that he never wanted to be released and
asked repeatedly to be allowed to die.

Both Rampton and Ashworth have received criticism in the past for their treatment of patients. In
1979, Yorkshire Television released a programme
titled *Rampton, The Secret Hospital,* showing the
severe mistreatment of Rampton patients by staff.
The show received an International Emmy, but
a follow-up a few weeks later found that its effect
had been less than desired. While a few scapegoats
had taken the fall for the problems highlighted, the
culture was largely as before, with the added diffi-
culty that staff no longer trusted one another as they
were concerned about whistle-blowing.

Following the impact of the programme, Sir John
Boynton led an inquiry in 1980, which made 205
recommendations on how to improve the hospital,
particularly its management. The inquiry called for
a body overseeing all institutions at which patients

were detained under the Mental Health Act, including Broadmoor and Ashworth, and set up review boards for each 'special hospital'.

After the death of a patient in 1988, Sir Louis Blom-Cooper set up the Committee of Inquiry into Complaints about Ashworth Hospital. Its findings, published in 1992, led to the dismissal of seven staff and two managers. Ashworth, like Broadmoor, was caught in the Jimmy Savile sex abuse scandal. Savile was reported to have sexually abused several patients there in the 1970s and 1980s.

After Savile, the Fallon Inquiry of 1998 is perhaps the most high-profile scandal to hit any of the three hospitals. In September 1996, an escaped inmate, Stephen Daggett, made a call from Dirty Harry's Bar in Amsterdam. Daggett, who was himself a convicted paedophile, claimed that the patients in the hospital had ready access to drugs, alcohol, and hardcore pornography, and that an eight-year-old girl had been making visits to a patient who was a convicted paedophile, and being allowed to play with him in a garden. The following inquiry, led by Peter Fallon, concluded Daggett's claims were almost entirely true.

Daggett had absconded from a day rehabilitation trip, after withdrawing £1,500 from his bank account and giving his nurse the slip. Once in Amsterdam, he said that he had absconded only as a way of drawing attention to his concerns, and promised to return to hospital if his claims were investigated. While Daggett did return to hospital, his claims were largely dismissed. It was not until Alice Mahon (then Labour MP for Halifax, where Daggett's parents lived) published his accounts that notice was taken. In light of this, a raid was ordered on Lawrence Ward, part of the Personality Disorders Unit. Its findings were startling. Not only was hardcore pornography in circulation amongst patients, it was available in the ward shop. More than 800 videos were found on the ward, including 225 videos in one patient's room alone, some of which contained bestiality and child abuse. Notably, some of these videos were in a medical cabinet that staff had no key for. Patients also had hidden stores of women's and children's underwear. Daggett made the outrageous claim in his phone call that room checks were hopeless, including his own nurse sitting on his bed reading porn and then clocking that as a room search!

Months after Daggett's whistle-blowing phone call, the eight-year-girl he had alleged was being allowed contact with patients who were a threat to her was taken into care. She was the child of a former patient of Ashworth. He had been taking her in to see Peter Hemming, who had been convicted of attempted rape of young girls, and Paul Corrigan, who had kidnapped, raped, and murdered a 13-year-old boy, John Haddon. It was after viewing Hemming bouncing the young girl on his knee while only in her underwear that Daggett felt the need to report this to the authorities.

The Fallon Inquiry of 1998 concluded though there was no evidence of abuse, the eight-year-old girl was being groomed for paedophilic purposes, and often spent time with the men completely unsupervised. It found, while on day leave, one of the two men had even been allowed to visit her at her home. According to the Inquiry, this 'disgraceful' situation was either ignored by the clinical staff or even believed to be for the patients' own good. Two successive chief executives resigned within two years of Daggett's explosive revelations.

The Fallon Inquiry concluded the management culture at the hospital was dysfunctional, that critical internal reports had been repressed, and that ministers had been misled about events at Ashworth.

It offered a total vote of no confidence in Ashworth Hospital and suggested it should close.

Following the Fallon Inquiry, Sir Richard Tilt reviewed the security of Ashworth and recommended it be upgraded to that of a Category B prison, one step below the maximum security of Category A. Daggett was afterwards moved to Rampton. Visits by children other than relatives of patients were completely banned. Six million pounds was invested in security at Ashworth, Broadmoor and Rampton, bringing in sniffer dogs, X-rays and metal detectors. Ashworth itself was given four months to develop an action plan for delivering urgent changes.

Inquiries such as Fallon and Blom-Cooper are part of the dark past of Britain's high security hospitals. The idea of abuse, inappropriate security, and ineffective management has left an indelible stain on public perception of the institutions. However, recent years have shown a marked improvement in the quality that the three hospitals have been able to offer. In their respective most recent CQC reports, the three hospitals each received 'Good' status and were found to be providing appropriate support.

OK, we said a very English scandal, but while there are only three high security mental health institutions in England and Wales, there is a fourth serving Scotland and Northern Ireland. Carstairs Hospital, based near the village of the same name in South Lanarkshire, Scotland, provides treatment for circa 140 patients. Like Broadmoor, it has come under criticism in recent years for low staffing levels.

Much like Broadmoor, Rampton and Ashworth, Carstairs has an alarm system that alerts nearby villages and towns of any patient escapes. All four hospitals have modelled their alarm systems on World War II air-raid sirens, and locals are kept well informed of when tests of the siren will be happening, to prevent fear.

Escapes have happened, though usually in the form of absconders on day release, rather than patients escaping from inside the prison itself. A notable exception to this is the break out by Robert Mone, who had shot dead a pregnant school teacher – Nanette Hanson – and sexually assaulted two teenage girls. Robert Mone was obsessed by another patient, Thomas McCulloch, in Carstairs for attempted murder. Mone had been a painter and decorator, and made a false wall in a cupboard, hiding weapons and a handmade ladder behind it.

On 30th November 1976, they both escaped, killing nurse Neil McLellan and another patient, Ian Simpson, in the process. The pair used axes and knives to kill the men with astonishing savagery. They then killed a police officer, George Taylor, and badly wounded another. The police had spotted them trying to hail a car outside the hospital after they escaped. They made a getaway in various cars but were eventually caught by police.

Neither returned to Carstairs, instead being imprisoned elsewhere. The judge who sentenced them for the murders said that they should never be released, but following a human rights appeal, McCulloch was released in 2003, his current whereabouts not publicly known.

In 2008, it was revealed that Carstairs had only one female patient, who therefore required a ward entirely to herself, costing £630,000 a year. Following this, in 2011, it was deemed that Carstairs should house only men. Then Chief Executive Andreana Adamson argued that women should not be subject to high levels of security because they pose less risk than men. Those women who would otherwise be in Carstairs were instead sent to medium security psychiatric units, or to one of the three high security facilities in England.

These accounts demonstrate a very similar trajectory to Broadmoor. All of these hospitals have moved on from outrageous incidents to a hugely better quality of care and safeguarding. It is also the same journey of far fewer people being diagnosed as criminally insane and large swathes of the patient population moving into prisons.

Chapter 15

The future for Broadmoor

For decades, concerns have been raised about Broadmoor's facilities. In 2003, the Commission for Health Improvement described the hospital as 'totally unfit for purpose'. Following eight suicides in as many years from 2001 to 2008, the hospital was ordered to improve facilities.

The design of Broadmoor's original Victorian buildings did not always turn out to be optimal for patient welfare. The T-shaped wards are barely usable, as they prevent lines of sight. This poses an increased suicide risk, and also prevents nurses from being able to care efficiently for patients. Most damningly, a 2009 CQC found Broadmoor's facilities to be completely inadequate and overcrowded. We were told time and again by staff that Broadmoor is really difficult to renovate. The buildings, many of which are over 150 years old, are listed buildings, and this level of protection means that they are incredibly difficult to undertake construction work on. In one particularly chilling example of the red tape this creates, when the hospital looked to remove window bars in order to prevent patients hanging themselves from them, they found that to do so would be illegal, due to the obvious historical significance of the buildings.

Finally, over 150 years after its doors opened, Broadmoor is moving house. In 2009, plans began for the hospital to uproot from its original Victorian site, where countless dramas have played out since 1863, and to move to a new, purpose-built hospital next door. It is a huge moment, possibly the biggest moment in Broadmoor's long and venerable history. The entire project was anticipated to cost in excess of £200million, and a preliminary, very optimistic moving-in date of June 2017 was suggested. The new Broadmoor has yet to open.

Although parts of the old buildings have been closed down or repurposed in the run-up to the move, there will be a moment when the old Broadmoor closes its doors for the very last time. What do key staff members and select patients feel about the move? As Pete Turner told us, 'The move to the new hospital will be a powerful moment.'

Strange as it sounds, there is plenty of nostalgia for the old hospital and all of its history. Both patients and staff have been involved in the decision-making on how the new premises will look and feel. Of course, the intention is that the new wards will be better ventilated, air-conditioned and rather more fragrant than the old Victorian wards and the stuffy 1970s additions. Most staff we asked about the move spoke highly of the redevelopment team at the new hospital.

Pat McKee has been an active participant within the redevelopment team. An enthusiastic cheerleader for the new hospital, he phrased this pivotal moment in history beautifully: 'In 1863, a new group of patients and staff walked into a state-of-the-art hospital. Now, a new group is doing that very first shift.'

Pat is full of praise for the layout of the new buildings. The new wards are light, bright and airy. Every ward will have its own gym equipment. There are three gardens in the new intensive care ward, to aid well-being. Each ward will have just ten to 12 patients, depending on the ward.

While the Victorian Broadmoor could not have been built with modern standards of patient care in mind, the new hospital is. In the new buildings, the whole place is purpose-built for technology, especially the central building. There is a free flow of lines of sight, which means no need for an escort. In the old hospital, accessible space for patients is limited to the terrace. That will all change. There is a glass-fronted shop, albeit shatterproof glass, hairdressers, cafes, and working areas.

We asked Pat what the patients' opinions of the new hospital were. Some, he said, were not interested because they will not be cared for at the hospital by the time the move happens; others are concerned they haven't physically seen it.

Pat described an art competition going on amongst the patients about the transition, to build enthusiasm and engagement in the project from the patient base. However, when asked whether any patients are likely to be able to physically see the hospital before they move, the answer was an indefinite maybe.

The new security control room and high secure perimeter access the latest technology. Lines of sight have been carefully enhanced across the campus, and ligature points diminished wherever possible. The new visitors centre will be much improved in terms of the experience that it offers.

A series of induction videos have been created for the patients to watch, too, as well as welcome packs. Once the wards had been carpeted, decorated, and all but ready to go, patients were able to see pictures of them. Having viewed these, patients said that they liked the look of the larger rooms and bedrooms, and the wet rooms. Several of the patients we met at the patient forum were especially pleased that they can regulate water temperature and room temperature in the new buildings.

It has not all been plain sailing. The Kier Group, a UK construction company with an annual revenue in excess of £4billion, has repeatedly pushed back its estimations of when the redevelopment of Broadmoor's new hospital will be completed. Just the phase-one block-building programme ended up being delivered 16 months late.

Kier have also ended up slipping on budget big time. The total capital cost of the project is projected at £249million and rising, at least £17million more than originally budgeted. Because of slow delivery on the project and concerns over the growing budget, the Hospital Redevelopment Board have retained consultancy company Arcadis since 2017 to oversee progress. On the flipside, the view taken by West London NHS Trust is that with patient safety always a priority, they can't move until they can be sure it is safe and secure.

While Kier leads on the construction of Broad-moor, Oxford Architects are taking the lead on designing and planning how the new hospital will look. Following an intensive appointment process, they began work on the project in 2009, initially predicting that it would be completed in its entirety by 2016.

Between these three companies, plans for the new Broadmoor are very slowly becoming reality. Parts of the new hospital have already been completed. The Paddock Centre, a 70-bed ward designed by Oxford Architects, was finished in 2005 at a cost of £25million.

Plans for the new hospital place it at a similar scale. With a footprint of 32,500m^2, it will provide wards and facilities for 234 patients, and Broadmoor came to Oxford Architects with briefs for the wards already developed. Oxford Architects, under Project Architect Rick Lamb and Partner Nick Caldwell, then created a brief for the Entrance Building, Central Building, perimeter security and secure external spaces.

Within these buildings and spaces they designed facilities for administration, shops, recreation, archive, canteen, visitors, group therapy, security and faith areas, consulting with clinicians, nurses,

psychiatrists, psychologists, estates, security, department heads and head of service in order to do so.
They also visited other mental health facilities in the
UK. That was the best way to see what worked well,
and what didn't.

The final concept for the design was based on
buildings surrounding a garden. The three wards
slant off from the strikingly beautiful Central Building, with a large stained-glass window designed with
input from patients and the chaplaincy. Central
Building, while not very originally named, will be the
central hub for all patient treatment and therapies,
as well as where administrative staff will be based,
while the three wards will obviously be for patient
accommodation. This is a change from the current
site, in which areas for rehabilitative work, admin
and patient living are intermingled throughout the
hospital, leaving staff often having to work in isolation from others in their team.

On top of the design focus on clear lines of sight,
large glass wall panels and CCTV will hopefully put
an end to the current level of observation and supervision required. The intention is to allow staff to focus
on treating their patients rather than just checking
up on them, as more time will then be allotted to

therapeutic activities. Each ward building roof will be topped with large Velux windows, which can open on a central pivot, creating areas that are not only well lit, but well ventilated, a far cry from the old Victorian T-shaped wards. Every detail has been considered, even the fitting of the bedroom windows, which are deliberately angled to allow in more light, but also to enhance privacy. A great deal of thought has gone into the artwork, the ceiling heights, the gardens and even the curtains, which are flame retardant.

It's not just the physical building that's being restructured, but the care pathway with it. The new focus is on a clear, measurable plan that sets out and promotes the route to recovery. The hope is that, in the new facilities, it will be easier for patients to undertake 'meaningful activity', which can include exercise, therapy, and the various workshops available, with each patient aiming to complete 25 hours a week in these areas.

We noticed that many hospital staff are using the move as a chance to examine and to improve their broader clinical practice. For instance, while security and care is 24/7, therapies and workshops exist only in the standard working day, five days a week, and discussions are currently in place as to whether these might be more effective were they also available in the evenings and at weekends.

Once the move to the new hospital is finally complete, the intriguing question remains of what is to be done with the original site. The intention is to sell off the old buildings and use this capital to help fund the new hospital. There has been talk amongst developers of Broadmoor being converted into luxury flats, and an apocryphal story about it being turned into Crowthorne's first luxury hotel, potentially themed around Broadmoor's gory history. What it would be perfect for is a filming location!

While any developers would be faced with the same listed building restrictions that have hamstrung Broadmoor staff for years, the hotel concept has been taken up elsewhere. In Oxford, it's possible to stay in the Malmaison, a converted former prison in which the cell rooms are now luxurious double rooms built from joining three cells rooms together, while the Karosta Prison Hotel in Latvia, formerly a KGB prison, trades off its dark past, advertising itself as 'unfriendly, unheated, uncomfortable'. Broadmoor's beautiful views, scenic local walks and golf courses and proximity to central London and Heathrow are all factors that make it potentially desirable as a hotel.

History buffs and preservation society members have been worried by the idea of converting Broadmoor into a hotel, arguing that doing so threatens the building's heritage. Many British government-owned buildings have been sold off over the years and fallen into disrepair and dereliction, including a number of historically significant hospitals. Many people would be desperately sad to see Broadmoor go the same way, including many of the hospital's own patients and staff, and us. Clive Bonnet and Pat McKee are particularly passionate exponents of the history of the old hospital, while acknowledging the many benefits of the new site.

Does it really make any sense to have a luxury hotel right next door to a high security hospital? Half of the pretty rural views would be over a functioning mental hospital. Not only does this raise concerns over security, but also the privacy of the patients.

Considering the lengths journalists have gone to in the past to secure photographs of patients such as Peter Sutcliffe, building a multi-storey building with potential sightlines into the complex is likely to worry staff, patients, and those who might visit them. There are plans in place that trees will be planted to screen the hospital from the hotel and vice versa:

this would be for aesthetic effect in addition to the intense security surrounding the new building itself. However, in an age of £50 drones that take little skill to fly, which have already been confirmed to be used to smuggle drugs into a number of different English prisons, this is unlikely to resolve all the problems this may raise.

Broadmoor Hospital these days is corporate. Well-run. Brimming with well-intentioned and risk-averse staff. The shift to the new site and the sale of the old buildings will not change that. As things stand, the fate of the iconic Victorian building, and its ultimate use or purpose, remains in doubt. There is even talk of doing away with the very name Broadmoor and all the sensationalist associations that come with it, if not now then in the foreseeable future.

Clive Bonnet marvelled that 'Broadmoor was the first *ever* high secure hospital when the Victorians built it. They couldn't have chosen a better site. A moor where you can see for miles. That's important, therapeutic. "I can see what I can be striving for," the patient thinks. "The *real* world is out there."'

He remembers being overwhelmed by a sense of permanence on his third shift in, walking up Upper Broadmoor Road: 'In 1946, when Dad started, they were telling him the place was finished. People always say that, but it is just *changing*. Broadmoor will never finish, Broadmoor is here forever.'

ACKNOWLEDGEMENTS

We want to thank Kelly Ellis, Justine Taylor and the whole amazing team at Bonnier Books UK. Our brilliant agents Martin Redfern and Diane Banks at Northbank Talent Management have been a source of wise counsel and encouragement throughout.

Sincere thanks to Leeanne McGee and Jimmy Noak for support, Gwen Adshead, Amlan Basu, Clive Bonnet, Pete Turner and Pat McKee for their engaging and insightful contributions.

Heartfelt thanks to the brilliant Alex King for his help in researching aspects of this book. Thanks to our parents Joy and Malcolm Levi and Angela and Roger French for all they have done through the years to help us to this point. Thanks to our children, families and friends for their patience.

Thanks most of all to the patients and staff that we have met, who shared their unique stories and Broadmoor experiences with us.